WILLIAM SAROYAN

BY ARAM SAROYAN

WILLIAM SAROYAN

by ARAM SAROYAN

Harcourt Brace Jovanovich, Publishers   San Diego · New York · London

Requests for permission to make copies of any
part of the work should be mailed to: Permissions,
Harcourt Brace Jovanovich, Publishers,
757 Third Avenue, New York, N.Y. 10017

Photograph on page 43 used by permission of
Saul Mauriber, executor of the Carl van Vechten
photographic collection.
Material contained in chapter 13 is adapted
from Last Rites by Aram Saroyan, published by
William Morrow & Co., Inc., and used
by their permission.

Library of Congress Cataloging in Publication Data
Saroyan, Aram.
William Saroyan.
Bibliography: p.
1. Saroyan, William, 1908–   —Biography.
2. Authors, American—20th century—Biography.
I. Title.
PS3537.A826Z89   1983
818'.5209   82–21313

ISBN 0–15–196762–8
        0–15–696780–4 (pbk.)

Designed by Joy Chu
Printed in the United States of America
First edition
B C D E

The division of life's determinants into the
"fatalities" of our constitution and the
"accidents" of our childhood may still be
indefinite in individual cases, but taken
altogether one can no longer entertain any
doubt about the precise importance of our
first years of childhood. We all still show
too little respect for nature, which, in
Leonardo's deep words recalling Hamlet's
speech, *is full of infinite reasons which never
appeared in experience.* Every one of us human
beings corresponds to one of the infinite
experiments in which these "reasons of nature"
force themselves into experience.

—Sigmund Freud,
Leonardo da Vinci

CONTENTS

Contents

ACKNOWLEDGMENTS

THIS biography of my father, William Saroyan, was undertaken at the suggestion of Matthew J. Bruccoli, who was also its editor. He gave me the freedom to develop the manuscript in my own way, and then offered incisively expert editorial insight to improve it. In short, this book would not exist but for him. Nor would it exist without the wholehearted support of my mother, Carol Matthau, who allowed me to be privy to the most intimate details of her relationship with my father. I know that her generosity opened old wounds, and yet she never once hedged in her willingness to let me write whatever I wanted to write. The love and trust she showed me make any expression of gratitude seem inadequate, but I am no less deeply grateful to her for that.

I would also like to acknowledge the generous help I received, in various phases of this project, from Armen Bagdasarian, Bruce Fisher, M.D., Dickran Kouymjian, Archie Minasian, Rosheen Marcus, Frank and Roxie Moradian, Stuart A. Robbins, Manuel J. Tolegian, Sanford Ungar, John Woods, and Andrew Wylie. Howard R. Floan's study, *William Saroyan* (New York: Twayne, 1966), repeatedly proved to be an invaluable resource.

A. S.

PREFACE

WILLIAM SAROYAN'S greatest fame, as well as his most enduring achievement as a writer, dates from the 1930s. As the *New York Times* put it in their front-page obituary on May 19, 1981: "Mr. Saroyan soared into the American consciousness in early 1934 with 'The Daring Young Man on the Flying Trapeze.' For the next decade, he dazzled, entertained and uplifted millions with hundreds of short stories and a series of plays . . ."[1]

Indeed, William Saroyan was one of those unique literary artists—like F. Scott Fitzgerald during the 1920s and Jack Kerouac in the late 1950s—who, at a certain point in the history of their society, come to personify—in a manner that quickly outstrips the strictly literary—what might be called the mythic potential of their particular social-historical moment.

In the 1980s, such a figure is far more likely to be a movie star than a writer, but in the period of Saroyan's greatest fame, the written word, especially as embodied in the short story form, was still in its prime as a popular medium, and a magazine like *Story*, which published Saroyan's first work, was capable of launching the writer as both a popular and a critical success.

In an astute obituary that appeared in the *Manchester Guardian*, W. J. Weatherby wrote: "For a time Saroyan was as much a literary public character as Hemingway, the American gossip columnists followed him about—but he lived long enough to find himself neglected . . ."[2] Indeed, in most of the obituaries for the writer in the English-language press, there is a discernible, if largely unspoken, bewilderment at the second half of his career.

For if William Saroyan was a sudden international celebrity at the age of twenty-six in 1934, by his death at seventy-two on May 18, 1981, he was known in his hometown, Fresno, California, as a reclusive, eccentric figure who kept a guarded distance from all but a few old friends. Three days after its obituary, the *Los Angeles Times* ran a second front-page piece on the writer's last years in Fresno, which noted that in Saroyan's neighborhood, where he had lived by himself on and off for the past seventeen years, "only the children have stories to tell. Their parents hardly knew the famous prize-winning novelist and playwright living in their midst."[3]

Most of the obituaries mentioned in passing the writer's two marriages to, and two divorces from, the New York debutante Carol Marcus—the first marriage having taken place in 1943 and the final divorce in 1951—and the *New York Times* went so far as to run this provocative excerpt from one of the writer's later memoirs: "Three years in the Army and a stupid marriage had all but knocked me out of the picture and, if the truth is told, out of life itself.

"Suicide was suicide, divorce was divorce. I flipped a coin, and it came up divorce."[4]

In several of the obituaries, there was also mention of problems with compulsive gambling and back taxes. In all of this, however, it was difficult for me, as the writer's son, to credit the press with anything more than the most tentative grasp of the reality of the second half of his life. And at the same time, given the writer's own work and public statements on the subject, it was hard to blame them for it. Only Weatherby in the *Guardian*, who had known Saroyan personally, called attention to the "shrewd peasant" side of the writer—a side that might go a long way, I think, in explaining the general bewilderment of the rest of the press.

It is one of the purposes of this study to tell more about the second half of William Saroyan's life than he himself told. I knew my father exclusively in this latter phase, and it has been a frustration of mine that his legend, dating back to the earliest part of his career, continues to dominate popular consciousness of both his literary career and his public image. It seems to me self-evident that his later life was as much the inevitable result of his character as were his years as a public legend. That his character, both as a writer and as a man, proceeded from the specific nature of his earliest experience and from his unique physical and psychological makeup is the central idea I have tried to explore in what follows.

ARAM SAROYAN
Bolinas, California

CHRONOLOGY

1908   William Saroyan is born in Fresno, California, on August 31, 1908, the fourth child of Armenak and Takoohi Saroyan, both Armenian immigrants.

1911   Armenak dies in San Jose, and Takoohi is forced to place her four children in the Fred Finch Orphanage in Oakland and take work as a domestic. Children remain in the institution for five years.

1916   Children return from the orphanage to a house Takoohi rents on San Benito Avenue in Fresno. Eight-year-old William sells the Fresno *Evening Herald* after school. Decides to become a writer after reading Guy de Maupassant's short story "The Bell." Drops out of school before completing the eighth grade. Delivers messages for the Postal Telegraph Company.

1926   Family moves to house on Carl Street in San Francisco. Saroyan works as a clerk, telegrapher, and then manager of a Postal Telegraph branch office.

1934   His short story, "The Daring Young Man on the Flying Trapeze," is published in the February issue of *Story* magazine to wide acclaim. He writes many stories and publishes widely. *The Daring Young Man on the Flying Trapeze and Other Stories* is published.

1935   Saroyan visits Soviet Armenia for the first time.

1939   *My Heart's in the Highlands* opens on Broadway in April and wins the Drama Critics Award for Best Play. *The Time of Your Life* opens in October.

1940   He wins both the Drama Critics Award and the Pulitzer Prize for *The Time of Your Life*, but rejects the Pulitzer Prize. *My Name Is Aram* is published.

1942   Saroyan meets Carol Marcus, a New York debutante, in Hollywood. He produces and directs his two plays *Across the Board on Tomorrow Morning* and *Talking to You* on Broadway; is inducted into the army at Sacramento.

1943   In February, he marries Carol Marcus in Dayton, Ohio, where he is stationed with the Signal Corps. His son, Aram, is born in September in New York. Soon afterward he is shipped overseas and stationed in London with the Film Unit of Signal Corps. *The Human Comedy* is published.

1945   Saroyan is honorably discharged from the army at Fort Lewis, Washington, in September, after thirteen months overseas duty. He settles with Carol and Aram in a house on Taraval Street in San Francisco.

1946   Birth of daughter, Lucy. *The Adventures of Wesley Jackson* is published.

1947   Plagued by compulsive gambling, he leases a house near Oyster Bay, Long Island, for six months. Returns with family to San Francisco.

1948   He rents apartment on East 58th Street in Manhattan.

1949   Saroyan divorces Carol Marcus in Reno. Visits Europe.

1951   Saroyan remarries Carol Marcus in Los Angeles; rents house on North Rodeo Drive in Beverly Hills. *Rock Wagram* is published.

1952   He divorces Carol Marcus in Santa Monica. Settles in Malibu while Carol and children live in Pacific Palisades.

1954   Carol moves with Aram and Lucy to Manhattan.

1960   Saroyan buys sixth-floor walk-up apartment in Opéra district in Paris. Purchases two adjacent tract houses in Fresno, California. Henceforth divides his year between his American and European homes. Writes series of memoirs.

1963   *Not Dying* is published.

1966   He forms the William Saroyan Foundation.

1979   Saroyan learns he has cancer of the prostate but decides against treatment. Publishes his final memoir, *Obituaries*. Makes will, leaving virtually his entire estate to the William Saroyan Foundation.

1981   In April, he is admitted to Veterans Administration Hospital in Fresno. Dies on the morning of May 18.

> ... the contempt of the past inevitably means
> that the self we have is more and more a
> fictive self ... for any true self is not only
> the result of a vital relation with a community
> but is also a development in time, and if there
> is no past there can be no self.
>
> —Robert Penn Warren,
> Democracy and Poetry

❦ PART ONE ❦

1

THE MAKING OF
AN ARTIST

T H I S is a book about a man who knew in his early teens that he wanted to be a writer, who acted on that knowledge by learning how to touch-type before dropping out of school for good, and who, although he came from a very poor family, felt so strongly about being a writer that he bought himself a typewriter with money that the family could have used for all sorts of other things, including food.

William Saroyan was a writer, or, as he himself might have written, a *writer*. He knew this very early in his life, and he knew it probably up to the very end of his life. The first question, then, might be just how and when this deepest and most enduring impulse of his life emerged.

.   .   .

BEFORE he was three years old, when his mind was still that of a prerational child, when he was just beginning to learn to talk, but before he could speak whole sentences—when he was, in fact, in the midst of *learning* the language that would give him his life's work—Saroyan experienced the deepest trauma of his life. His Armenian immigrant father, Armenak, died of a ruptured appendix in San Jose, California, and his mother, Takoohi, was forced to put him, along with her three older children, into an orphanage for the next five years.

TO survive such an experience at so vulnerable an age, some sort of major psychic adjustment is inevitable, and in Saroyan's case it is not unlikely that this reaction is related to his subsequent desire—it might even be called his compulsion—to write. Indeed, such a primary experience so early in his life may have caused a personal transformation, a fundamental interior shift, that provided both the psychic and physical groundwork that enabled the child to grow into an artist of a specific order.

The very young child's nervous system, with all its natural responsiveness, can be compared to a woodland lake that reflects everything in its clear depths. Suddenly, however, this lake, reflecting everything in its quiet embrace, is subjected to an abrupt and totally unexpected change of season. The death of Armenak and Saroyan's subsequent five years in the Fred Finch Orphanage in Oakland was comparable to the onrush of a fierce and seemingly unending winter.

How did Saroyan psychologically survive this long siege, coming as it did smack in the middle of his first six years, and lasting right through and beyond them—the very years Freud tells us are the most critical in determining the human psychological makeup? When he left the orphanage with his brother and sisters to live with his mother in the little house she had managed to provide for them in Fresno, Saroyan had in fact spent most of his life in an institution.

In a sense, it would not be inaccurate to say that the child survived this period of his life in a manner more or less parallel to the way the lake would survive its winter—by freezing. Or perhaps, in his case, it would be more accurate to say that he crystallized. For in freezing, his surface and interior did not become opaque and impenetrable. He remained, like the lake, a reflecting mirror—but the consistency of his inner nature had changed. It was no longer fluid. It was hard now, like a glass mirror. And in just this sense, perhaps, he became a potential artist.

This is not to imply that all anybody needs in life to grow up to become a Pulitzer Prize-winning author is to be forced by circumstances into an orphanage at a critical moment in early childhood.

Statistics are eloquent in refuting any such notion. Indeed, there are most likely an infinite number of responses to such a crisis in early childhood, and even among those who, however involuntarily, seize upon the response of an interior freeze, the odds must be a million to one against this freeze "taking" without leaving both the surface and the interior of the child to some extent opaque, uncommunicative—damaged in some way. What happened in Saroyan's case was, in its way, as unlikely as a whole lake freezing over while still continuing not just to reflect its surroundings but, should someone gaze into its depths, to reveal the flora and fauna of its interior life at the very moment of its freezing.

S A R O Y A N was, from all reports, an extremely lively, energetic, and intelligent child—and a deeply imaginative one. He seemed unburdened by his early misfortune, and his teachers at Emerson School in Fresno immediately recognized that here was a force to contend with. He scored way above average on the school's IQ test, and in the classroom he was a witty and rambunctious character, his pace often obviously too quick for the class as a whole. He was a boy who could take his turn as class cut-up, but perhaps more gladly still laughed at his fellow class cut-ups.

Why claim, then, an interior difference for a child who seemed at least as capable as any of his peers in whatever he attempted? It should be stressed that there may have been no evidence of any disability whatever. On the contrary, it is possible that Saroyan's comparative hardness, which in his case entailed no corresponding loss of clarity—like that crystalline lake—might in a sense *guarantee* his intelligence. In effect, he could remain unruffled by circumstances to a degree impossible for contemporaries who had experienced no equivalent interior alchemy, who were still fluid inside, and therefore were subject to emotional upsets where Saroyan's depths would remain undisturbed.

He was, then, almost from the beginning, an *observer*. He watched. He laughed. Occasionally, he would join the ruckus or match his wit against the teacher's, but such contests were usually hurriedly terminated by the teacher ordering Saroyan off to the principal's office.

AFTER school, selling newspapers at his corner in downtown Fresno, he observed the human comedy in its urban variety. Across the street from his corner was a movie house to which he was frequently admitted free to watch parts of Charlie Chaplin movies. One evening, as he came out of the theater with a favorite cousin after watching a reel in which little Charlie had booted a large woman in her rear in a fracas, he was amazed when the cousin, a bit younger than he, attempted the same stunt there on the twilit Fresno street corner, only to be severely rebuked, physically as well as verbally, by the woman he had chosen for his target.

Saroyan, imaginative as he was, would never have been so caught up by a movie, or any other form of art, that he would mistake it for real life or be lured into such impulsive mischief by it. Even as a boy, Saroyan had about him a strong and self-protective propriety—a kind of fundamental "street smarts"—and, although he would later have his day as the *enfant terrible* of the American theater, that trait was of the very essence of his character.

He was a man who made his own obeisance to convention, to the received wisdom of his day; surprisingly, perhaps, he lacked the conviction of authentic rebellion. Indeed, his protest was mostly of the nose-thumbing variety, part and parcel of a repertory of bad-boy antics that was more a dimension of his art or his public persona than any deeper, more risky impulse.

For almost from the very beginning, he would tend to look into life, rather than surrender himself spontaneously to it. He was to be an outsider, in this deepest sense, perhaps because being an *insider* would have meant unfreezing, melting, letting the ice turn back into water, and this transformation would remain almost always beyond him during the main course of his life.

THE reasons Saroyan focused so early and with such certainly on his ambition to become a writer are, perhaps, both less arbitrary and more complicated than might at first be thought.

As a young child, he believed that books were quite literally written by God. The two realizations that they were, after all, written by mortals and that he wanted to write them seem to have occurred more or less simultaneously. Apparently, in the very moment he understood that such an undertaking was available as a life choice, he knew it was the life for him. How was that possible for a child scarcely nine or ten years old? To begin with, literal association of the written word with God's word seems to have been the single instance of Saroyan's being less advanced, less savvy, than his age might warrant, and because the rest of the evidence all points the other way, it might be surmised that there was something personally willful and self-fulfilling in this delusion.

T H E return from the orphanage was not a return to life as he had known it before his incarceration. He returned to a fatherless home; and it isn't difficult to imagine that in the intervening years, during which Takoohi had been forced to work as a domestic, his young and pretty mother had hardened under her burden.

Saroyan told of returning home from school one afternoon and being asked by a neighborhood boy to join in a game of baseball. He knew he had newspapers to sell, but nevertheless he joined the game instead of going to his job. After playing briefly outside his house, he heard Takoohi calling him and left the game to go to her.

"What are you doing?" she asked him.

"Playing," he replied, knowing that, at least for the boys whose game he had joined, it was the most natural answer in the world.

Saroyan's mother's family came from a town in Armenia known as Bitlis, now a part of Turkey, and these people are known throughout Armenia for their proud and scornful nature—for their toughness.

"Playing?" Takoohi said, as though she had not heard him correctly.

"Yes . . . ," he answered, "baseball . . ."

"Baseball?" Takoohi repeated slowly, now with broad sarcasm and unmistakable scorn. The young boy quickly reported to work after this failed experiment.

He was not like other boys. He was not permitted some of their more pleasant options, even after his return from the orphanage. And perhaps the most obvious difference between him and his contemporaries was that he lacked a father, someone to take care of him and the rest of his family, including Takoohi.

.   .   .

H E had almost no memory of Armenak. There were several photographs of the man, both alone and with his family, and he bore a look that was altogether different from most of the other immigrant Armenians of Fresno. Handsome and proud in bearing, with a large old-country mustache, there was yet something unsettled about him, a suggestion of the erratic. Even in his mid-thirties, he still had the large eyes of a startled child.

Armenak had not come from Bitlis. He was from a softer, gentler tribe of Armenians. He was remembered very affectionately by those who had known him, but there was an unmistakable note of disappointment, sometimes almost of derision, in this affection. The man had been a dreamer— perhaps, in his own way, superior to many who had survived long after he himself had perished; but what was the good of that kind of superiority in such times as these and in such a place as this?

Saroyan was even told that his father had been the most wonderful man of all the Armenians of Fresno. But at the same time, he knew at first hand the punishment his father's death had visited on his family.

And Armenak's death itself was not without its equivocal, almost willful, dimension.

H E had come to America just after the turn of the century to start a new life and, as soon as he was able, to send for his family—his wife, Takoohi, and their three children.

Armenak arrived in the new world already an ordained minister of the Armenian Orthodox Church, and his command of English was so sure that he soon established a warm friendship with a Presbyterian minister in New York City named William Stonehill. Then he was hired to head the Armenian Orthodox parish in Paterson, New Jersey.

O N C E Takoohi and the children had arrived, the family set up a home in Paterson. William, the last of Armenak and Takoohi's children, and the only one to be conceived and born in America, was named after Armenak's friend, the Reverend Stonehill.

Most of Takoohi's relatives from Bitlis had chosen to make their homes in Fresno, clear across the continent, and, uprooted as this young woman must have felt in the new world, it wasn't long before she was

Armenak Saroyan. New York. 1907.

speaking to her husband of making the move to California, where they would know so many of the Armenians already settled there and where the climate was apparently so similar to their part of Armenia. Armenak, on the other hand, having had the good luck to find a large and challenging parish, wasn't as eager to move. Then, according to family lore, a letter arrived from Fresno Armenians with the good news that a parish had been located for Armenak, that he could have his own church there, too. Whatever misgivings Armenak might have had before were now set aside, and the family decided to make the move.

EVIDENCE of the closeness of Armenak's relationship with the Stonehills was provided over two decades later. Saroyan, now an aspiring young writer of twenty, had borrowed $100 from his Uncle Mihran, Armenak's brother, to make a trip across the country by bus so that he could see New York. While he was on the East Coast, he made a pilgrimage to Paterson, New Jersey, to see his long-dead father's church, and he also paid a call at the New York home of the Stonehills. He had not written ahead that he would be coming. Mrs. Stonehill opened her front door, took one look at this young stranger who had been named after her husband, and, before he could introduce himself, she said "You are Armenak Saroyan's boy."

THE parish in Fresno turned out to be a ruse or a lie or maybe just a sad disappointment. Apparently, there was some sort of church and some sort of parish; but the church was a ramshackle affair at best and the parish poor and small. It was quickly apparent that Armenak would have to seek some other way to make a living. And so, at around the halfway mark of his life, this man was called upon to commit himself to some bold new course of action. Having reached that time of life when one's chosen path should be familiar and comfortable enough to begin to yield its expected benefits, Armenak found himself deprived of these rewards.

Another sort of man might have made this moment yield an unexpected fulfillment. But that would most likely have taken a younger man or one less spiritually volatile than the man Armenak seems to have been. Those eyes seem to speak of a need for slow and steady progress through life—a need to be deeply committed to this vocation lest he lose touch with the deeper values that steady a person's worldly endeavor. Armenak was an ordained minister and a poet, choices that speak of a strong inner need to keep to his own center.

Suddenly now, and irrevocably, he was compelled to be someone else. In this new country, which lacked the hallmarks of a genuine culture, slowly accrued over generations, but which was instead, almost by definition, the very opposite: a nation created and settled by a theory of piecemeal investment, a kind of vast crazy-quilt of financial designs—in such a country and time, this man found himself suddenly lost. He needed to throw away his whole life, like a thirty-five-year-old mistake, and start over again.

And that is what he did: Armenak Saroyan took up chicken farming. Then, one hot summer afternoon in the town of Campbell, where the family had moved, he was carried into the house by two neighbor men and put down on a sofa from which he was never to rise under his own power. The men left Armenak to the care of his wife, Takoohi, while they went for a surrey to transport him to the hospital in San Jose. It looked to be appendicitis.

Armenak was parched and pleaded with Takoohi to bring him a glass of water. Takoohi knew that water would only aggravate the appendicitis, if that is what it was, but here she was, looking at the flushed and fevered brow of the man she had loved since girlhood, whom she had seen reduced to circumstances that had driven the light from his eyes. And now he wanted something again. He wanted water. He pleaded with her. She resisted.

But her husband's pleas eventually wore her down. Perhaps she knew, deep within her, that Armenak wanted to die: that his pleading was in fact for deliverance, that his real thirst was for extinction.

And, in the end, perhaps for the very reason that she loved him—and in their photographs together she looks like a woman in love—she showed him mercy. She brought him his glass of water. He was allowed to drink, to slake his thirst. And then to die.

It didn't take long for his appendix to burst. When he knew he was dying, he summoned himself back out of delirium into the room—into life— one final time, to say the last words he would say to his wife, who would now have to go on alone without him. "Takoohi," he told her, "don't beat the children." Then he was gone.

ABOVE: *From l. to r.: Aram, Lucy, Henry, Verkine, Zabel, Takoohi, and Cosette Saroyan. Le Havre. 1906.*

LEFT: *Cosette, Takoohi, Henry, Zabel. Le Havre. 1906.*

ABOVE: *Zabel, Takoohi, Henry, Armenak, and Cosette Saroyan. New York. 1907.*

RIGHT: *At top, Mrs. William Stonehill; at bottom, Cosette Saroyan. New York. 1907.*

. . .

THIS is the pivotal moment in the story of Saroyan's childhood, and it is fraught with the deepest ambiguity. Did Armenak want to die? There is at least a hint of that possibility. And Saroyan was fated to wrestle with the implications of such a possibility all his life. For he discovered while still a child, before the age of reason, what terrible consequences such an impulse to die could have.

At the time, however, he could not have understood the situation, except to sense the terror implicit in it for all of the family. He would come to know the death scene only by hearsay. Once he had reached the age when he could be told the story of his father's death, it would be described to him. But by that time, the *fact* of this death had already imprinted itself deep within his nervous system. It was a part of him before he could give it a name. Lacking the link of language, a young child sees his world namelessly; and death without a name proved to be the most powerful and fundamental experience of Saroyan's life.

IT wasn't until near the end of his life that Saroyan could actually bring himself to write of the particulars of his orphanage experience; and he did it only after others had prompted him, urging upon him the importance of the experience in his own development. During the final years of his life, in fact, Saroyan made the rather remarkable discovery that his orphanage experience had lasted for *five* years, instead of the *three* he had imagined it to be all his life.

If one keeps in mind that these events occurred when he was in the very midst of learning language, it seems probable that the bonding function of language became even more critical for this child, whose own mother and father had vanished in the middle of the language-learning process.

MOREOVER, for such a child, whose own emotional fluency may have, at the deepest levels, been checked, words might become a way of reanimating his own frozen core. It seems more than incidentally significant that the story Saroyan said moved him to decide to become a writer was "The Bell" by Guy de Maupassant, which tells of the life of a multiple amputee on the streets of Paris. Maupassant's tale deals with a man who is physically, rather than psychically, immobilized, but the parallel is striking.

*Mihran, Armenak, William, and Takoohi
Saroyan. Fresno. 1909.*

*Zabel, Henry, William, and Cosette
Saroyan. California. c. 1910.*

Henry and William Saroyan just after Armenak's death. Campbell, California. 1911.

.   .   .

THE crucial evidence for the psychic freeze, however, would appear to lie in Saroyan's own writing, where there is essentially only a single character, the author himself. To read Saroyan is to commune with this voice.

Even in the most genuinely novelistic of his books, *The Human Comedy* (1943), almost all of the central characters may be regarded as versions of the author himself in various chronological incarnations: Ulysses, the child who sees the world in wordless wonder; Homer, the schoolboy and Postal Telegraph messenger, who gets to know the world through his job, delivering words in the form of telegrams—and, in one of the novel's most powerful scenes, words of death; Mr. Spangler, the young bachelor and manager of the Postal Telegraph office, perhaps a version of the writer himself at the time, the *word manager* (Saroyan had been the youngest manager of a Postal Telegraph office in the country in his early twenties); and even William Grogan, the old night-shift telegraph operator, the novel's kindly father figure, whose death occurs as he is typing up a telegram from the war department to inform Homer's mother of the death of his older brother, Marcus. This final character might be said to embody the deathly, spectral dimension of life that Armenak's death impressed on Saroyan's consciousness.

The same might be said of the central characters in his most celebrated play, *The Time of Your Life*. Perhaps most remarkable here is the relationship between Joe, the barroom philosopher, and his friend Tom, the childlike innocent who runs errands for Joe, catering to his every whim, because he is seemingly dependent on Joe to keep him out of trouble.

What is fascinating in these works is not the depiction of realistic characters and their relationships. There is something abstracted and dreamlike about almost all of Saroyan's figures and their central relationships. What fascinates rather is the *movement* from character to character, often recorded in their exchanges with one another, which frequently resemble an imaginative equivalent of the dynamic psychic interactions Freud described among the superego (the parent figure), the ego (the adult), and the id (the child).

Perhaps Saroyan's psychic freeze at the age of three allowed him to maintain these psychic archetypes as they lived in him at the moment of freezing. Thus, in his books we see the world quite literally through the eyes of a child. At the same time, in projecting characters who are drawn essentially from his own psychological makeup, rather than from the world at large, the writer performs a godlike miracle. He *reanimates* his own frozen interior: he brings himself back to life.

RETURNING to the image of the frozen lake, one may observe what is perhaps the primary characteristic of Saroyan's art. The writer was able to reflect his surroundings, even at their most threatening, without becoming personally overwhelmed by them. When a stone drops into the water, the whole surface of the lake is affected, altering in turn the image the lake reflects. But a frozen lake will continue to reflect its surroundings, and even when a stone drops on its surface, no very significant change occurs.

In 1934, at the age of twenty-six, Saroyan suddenly became a famous writer when his first story, "The Daring Young Man on the Flying Trapeze," appeared. The subject of this story was a penniless young writer who eventually succumbs to starvation and dies in San Francisco in the midst of the Great Depression.

Yet despite the melancholy subject matter of the story and certain parallels between its hero's and Saroyan's own life at the time, the style of the writing has an almost childlike lyricism, a strange buoyancy in its portrayal of the dying young writer; and the final lines, in which the young man is transformed by death, are grandly transcendent in their poetry:

> Then swiftly, neatly, with the grace of the young man on the trapeze, he was gone from his body. For an eternal moment he was all things at once: the bird, the fish, the rodent, the reptile, and man. An ocean of print undulated endlessly and darkly before him. The city burned. The herded crowd rioted. The earth circled away, and knowing that he did so, he turned his lost face to the empty sky and became dreamless, unalive, perfect.[1]

William Saroyan's career as a writer began with this image of death amidst social and economic cataclysm. Yet sad and moving as the story was, it was also strangely uplifting and ennobling. Written in and about the American Depression, it was, paradoxically, not fundamentally sorrowful.

But in light of Saroyan's earliest experience, perhaps this is less surprising than it might otherwise be. In effect, he had been handling his own personal, human equivalent of the Depression since before he was three years old. This condition was prevalent in society at the time his abilities as a writer matured to the extent that he was able to produce a finished and remarkable work of art. The result was this very personal story almost at once became a popular symbolic reflection of the state of the entire society. And he was famous.

2

THE DARING YOUNG MAN ON THE FLYING TRAPEZE

A M O N G Armenak's effects were several notebooks of his writings, including his poetry, in Armenian. Saroyan never made very much of these writings. He couldn't read Armenian, although he could speak it. If any of this writing was ever read aloud to him by his mother or someone else, or if he ever endeavored to have any of it translated for him, it apparently made very little impression on him. I know of no specific poems or texts that Armenak ever wrote—and this was the sort of thing my father might ordinarily have been expected to be interested in and to speak about to his own family. Very likely he *was* interested in the fact that Armenak had written *something*, and that it had remained unpublished, but preferred to leave the specifics of this writing be. He had almost no real memories of his father. He was left with the image of the kind and gentle, but apparently rather weak, man that was passed on to him by relatives and others who had known Armenak.

T H E older male figures in his writings are usually of that variety known as dreamers, human castoffs of one sort or another. Jasper McGregor, the old man with the bugle in his first produced play, *My Heart's in the Highlands*, and Kit Carson, the lovable teller of tall tales in *The Time of Your Life*, come to mind, in addition to Mr. Grogan in *The Human Comedy*. These characters, weak and downtrodden (though colorful) as they often are, lend a poetic dimension to the writings in which they appear that is essential to the charm of Saroyan's work. They are weak, but nevertheless vital, links to the past, to history and to tradition, within the accelerated present tense of the American landscape.

The old Arab in *The Time of Your Life*, a sterner old man than these others, is identifiably an old-world character, one who never attempted to become Americanized. His single line in the play, which occurs in periodic counterpoint to the main dramatic action, is the bleak and telling pronouncement: "No foundation—all the way down the line."

I F this was indeed the reality of the American scene, then Saroyan had gained the most intimate personal knowledge of its truth from the events of his own life. How was the lack of a father, which in a certain sense was the American condition at large—its dissociation from any genuine historical or geographical continuity—to be made up for in one's own sense of self? For Saroyan, the answer seems to have been, almost from the beginning, by writing. And here his early illusion that books were written by God reveals its personally prophetic dimension, since writing may have been the means by which he quickened and completed a self that might have otherwise been condemned by its earliest experience to a psychic rigor mortis.

I S it possible that in the very act of writing Saroyan may have felt some sense of communion with his long-departed father? In becoming a writer, he had taken up a primary but unfulfilled dimension of his father's life, and through his effort and persistence, he brought it to a large and, to all those around him, totally unexpected fulfillment. In doing what his father did and becoming a success at it, he might be said, on the one hand, to have vindicated Armenak, and on the other to have usurped his father's place in his own person. In these terms, his lack of curiosity about his own father's writing makes sense. He seems to have decided very early on to forego any close study of Armenak and to seek instead to assume for himself the role of writer—and ultimately, perhaps, in good American style, to *improve* upon it. In this sense, he became his own father. His lack of interest in Armenak might also have had an element of fear in it, fear that too close a study could infect him with Armenak's failure.

THIS attitude toward his immediate past is at once at the heart of Saroyan's achievement as a writer and may be, at the same time, an example —in bold personal relief—of the terms of the bargain struck by many Americans with their own history. The whole idea of the new world was a new start. And if one were to become a success in America, one had best look forward and not back. For in the past lay all the errors and outright nightmares that had led to the state of historical disjuncture that was, almost by definition, the American reality. Here, suddenly, unshackled of historical precedent, anything was possible—if one only had the will, and the nerve. Just as the blind develop extraordinary hearing to compensate for their missing faculty, so Americans, having turned their backs on their past, seemed to develop a powerful compensatory capacity to hasten the future forward.

THERE is the example of Saroyan's uncle, Aram Saroyan, Takoohi's younger brother,* who had come over on the boat from Armenia with his sister and her children. At the time, Aram was only a boy of twelve, but there was already a shrewd look about him, and he soon established himself among the men on the ship as an astute gambler.

Once in the new world, Aram wasted little time getting ahead. Perhaps, in part, his advantage lay in his age. Unlike Armenak, his time in his native country had been too brief to establish his character. He arrived in America young enough to become an American himself. And he went about this personal transformation with undisguised relish.

By the time Saroyan got out of the orphanage, Aram was a grown

---

* Takoohi's maiden name was Saroyan, too, although she and Armenak were not related.

man. He eventually became a Fresno success as a criminal lawyer, known for his ability to win over juries with his impassioned summaries, apparently sometimes on behalf of the guilty. Of all the Armenians in Fresno of his day, Uncle Aram rapidly became the most celebrated. Uncle Aram was also the most readily available male role model in the world Saroyan entered after the orphanage—and the impact of this fact on his subsequent development would be difficult to overestimate. Here was a man of power, eloquence, and dramatic physical magnetism, yet, at the same time, one with something obviously coarse and sometimes even cruel about him. The new world, for Aram, seems to have been an immense game, for which, as often as possible, he liked to make up his own rules.

SAROYAN'S attitude toward his Uncle Aram was as ambivalent, in its way, as his attitude toward his father. The two were, in fact, polar opposites that he would forever attempt to reconcile in his own person. What he learned from and respected in Aram was the man's courage and mastery in the moment—and a gift for spontaneous comic invention. At the same time, another side of Saroyan, the part of him allied with Armenak, abhorred Aram's unscrupulous character. The man didn't hesitate to play havoc with values traditional among Armenians—honesty and rigorous moral probity being chief among them.

These were, then, the two primary sides of Saroyan's own character. During his lifetime, it would prove virtually impossible for him ever to approach an objective assessment of the character and value of either Armenak's or Aram's life. In one sense, any such assessment would have been beside the point. For limited and imperfect as both of them might prove to be, he needed them: each was essential to his own identity. Even if their individual impulses might at times have been absolutely contradictory, there was to be no lasting coming to terms with either man—not in Saroyan's deeper self, not for a man who had been orphaned before the age of three.

IF his orphanage experience had effected a kind of psychological freeze, there is evidence from Saroyan's earliest history after the orphanage of a personal emphasis on *speed*, of a delight in accelerated physical *mobility* in general, that might be regarded as a compensation for the immobilization of his deeper reality.

Saroyan's uncle Aram as a watermelon salesman. San Francisco. 1913.

Aram Saroyan as a criminal lawyer. 1932.

Uncle Aram (second from left) *as a member of Fresno High School Senate. 1914.*

At the age of eight, he was among the fastest newsboys in Fresno, relishing the daily contest of ridding himself of his afternoon papers at his corner before his cohorts. A few years later, he was known to be the fastest Postal Telegraph messenger on bicycle in the entire San Joaquin Valley.

SAROYAN once told of an accident he had one afternoon in Fresno while delivering telegrams on his bicycle. He had ridden swiftly up to a cross street, only to be stopped abruptly by a policeman directing traffic from the center of the intersection. He slammed on his brakes at the policeman's signal, but the driver behind him wasn't as quick in his response as he was and rammed into the back of the bicycle. On impact, he found himself literally flying through the air above the traffic cop, his bicycle left crumpled behind him. In describing this moment of flight, which for him took place in a kind of slow motion, Saroyan remarked with delight at how the traffic cop looked up at him in wonder as Saroyan passed over him in the middle of the intersection and, at the same time, at how he himself looked down in midflight with equal wonder at the cop.

Somehow or other, in the midst of the accident, there was a moment of unexpected communion: a mute and awestruck acknowledgment on the part of both the policeman and the messenger of the endless capacity of life to surprise, creating for both of them a momentary breach in reality, an opening to a dimension of the eternal. In retrospect, this moment might be regarded as a prophetic glimpse into Saroyan's future: an initial and very physical rehearsal for the daring young man on the flying trapeze, who seems to defy space and time while he communicates gracefully under pressure and creates a moment of magic between himself and his audience.

This emphasis on speed and mechanical mobility was also to play its role in Saroyan's commitment to becoming a writer. Having made his decision, his first step was to switch from Longfellow Junior High to Technical High in Fresno so that he could take typing and shorthand. Once he had learned these, he dropped out of school for good, not yet having completed the eighth grade.

His next step was to save his money in order to buy his own typewriter, which he seems to have considered indispensable for pursuing his literary ambition. Armenak's notebooks had been handwritten in a foreign

Saroyan as a postal telegraph messenger. Fresno. c. 1920.

Saroyan (third from left) with his cousins Helen, Archie, and Kirk Minasian. Fresno. 1920. (Photograph courtesy of Archie Minasian.)

language. From the very beginning, Saroyan himself seems to have decided to produce clean, typed copy that could immediately be put up for sale in the literary marketplace.

DURING the following ten years, he received many rejection slips, but all the while he was evolving an approach to writing that applied the same standards of clarity and professional expertise he had brought to the strictly mechanical side of his art from the outset.

Saroyan was eventually to create a prose style that was, in its own way, an example of the American genius for invention. He learned to write extremely swiftly, with an easy-natured clarity and economy of means— like the "clean lines" of the new American cars or skyscrapers—and at the same time his prose developed a rhythm, an almost palpable beat, that reflected the complex acceleration of American life.

As this style was gradually taking shape in Saroyan's writing, America itself was moving inexorably toward social and economic catastrophe. As he worked to perfect his fluency in his chosen medium, the country was getting closer and closer to an unprecedented breakdown: the economic crash of 1929 and the ensuing years of the Great Depression.

IN 1933, just before he wrote the breakthrough story that would bring his name to the world, Saroyan completed a novel called "Trapeze over the Universe" that was entirely made up of the kind of stream of consciousness writing he would use in the first section of "The Daring Young Man on the Flying Trapeze."

He was, by this time, to all of his family and relatives, a confirmed misfit. Having risen to office manager in his Postal Telegraph job, after a few years he abruptly decided to quit this job and devote his full energies to writing. To those closest to him, this was the act of a lunatic.

The family had moved in 1926 to the house at 348 Carl Street in San Francisco, and his brother and two sisters all had jobs. Each morning at breakfast, Saroyan's older brother Henry would give him a dime so that he could take a streetcar downtown to the Main Branch of the San Francisco Public Library in the afternoon after his day's writing and then take one back to Carl Street again that evening.

Takoohi seems to have indulged her youngest child from the sense that such aberrant behavior was more or less helpless on his part, the inevitable result of his character, recalling for her earlier members of the family who had been similarly "touched." Although Henry helped each day with the dime, he otherwise seems not to have been very encouraging; and Saroyan's two older sisters, Cosette and Zabelle, were scornful and troubled, respectively. Cosette would sometimes loudly and sternly berate the young writer for his foolishness, while Zabelle, who of all the family was closest to him, once burned a bundle of his early stories because she felt ashamed for him after reading them.

But of all the family, it was Uncle Aram who was most visibly angered by the young man's determination not to work at anything other than writing. Perhaps, since he was the father substitute for the whole family, this was only natural. Uncle Aram was so outraged one afternoon by what he saw as Saroyan's shameless willingness to live without making his own fair contribution to the family finances that he tried to throw him bodily out of his own house, and would have succeeded had it not been for Takoohi, who told him to leave her son alone.

THIS early novel, "Trapeze over the Universe," which Saroyan thought highly enough of to have two copies—the original and first carbon—bound by a Chinese bookbinder he knew (they were mistakenly bound, Chinese fashion, "backwards"), seems to have been a "letting go" for him, after the endless toil and discipline of his apprentice years. (His first published story had appeared in the August 1928 issue of *Overland Monthly and Out West Magazine*.)

At the same time, it was this writing that directly preceded his breakthrough into the style that would make his name. Perhaps it reintroduced the vital dimension of freedom which his discipline had suppressed. There were whole pages in the book that were simply an unpunctuated succession of words, sometimes uninterrupted nouns: "rock tree alphabet mile soup injustice night . . ."

In a way, it was like a book of night. It was the other side of the daylight world, Armenak's side rather than Aram's, which he seemingly needed to reinstate fully before he could take his first full step into literature, knowing both the dark and the light, Armenak and Aram, and the rhythm by which they alternate: sleep and wakefulness, day and night, life and death, the rhythm of the planet itself: "Helplessly his mind sang, *He flies through the air with the greatest of ease; the daring young man on the flying trapeze.*"[1]

A N D there he was, suddenly launched over the whole of America, the daring young man, moving from "SLEEP" to "WAKEFULNESS," as he divided the two parts of his story, the first part written in the same style he had used throughout "Trapeze over the Universe," but now punctuated, given flesh, rhythmically pulsing with the music that perhaps the knowledge and acceptance of both sides of himself had set singing in him. The story began:

> Horizontally wakeful amidst universal widths, practicing laughter and mirth, satire, the end of all, of Rome and yes of Babylon, clenched teeth, remembrance, much warmth volcanic, the streets of Paris, the plains of Jericho, much gliding as of reptile in abstraction, a gallery of watercolors, the sea and the fish with eyes, symphony, a table in the corner of the Eiffel Tower, jazz at the opera house, alarm clock and the tap-dancing of doom, conversation with a tree, the river Nile, Cadillac coupe to Kansas, the roar of Dostoyevsky, and the dark sun.[2]

The second part of the story is focused on the writer, awake now, whose sleep has been embodied in the story's first section—and this young man, with a kind of lightheaded gaiety, is starving to death.

" T H E Daring Young Man on the Flying Trapeze," published in the February 1934 issue of *Story* magazine, is a kind of transmutation of Armenak's story of failure, set in the present day of his son William's America, with the hero bearing a closer resemblance to the writer than to his father. And Saroyan follows this young man (his father's side of himself, as it were) as he gradually awakens to an awareness of his fate: "It was then that he became thoroughly awake: at the thought of dying. Now wakefulness was a state in the nature of a sustained shock. A young man could perish rather unostentatiously, he thought . . ."[3]

He goes to an employment agency for an interview but there is no work. He walks to the YMCA, where he begins to compose on its free stationery "An Application for Permission To Live." After an hour, growing faint from the bad air in the place and from hunger, he leaves and walks to Civic Center Park across from the Public Library, where "he drank almost a quart of water and felt himself refreshed."[4] He now enters the Public Library and reads Proust for an hour: "then, feeling himself to be swimming away again, he rushed outdoors. He drank more water at the fountain in the park and began the long walk back to his room."[5]

T H E trapeze, swinging back and forth between the young man's poetic fancy and the brutal facts of his reality, is now suspended above a specific world, above America (instead of the broader "universe" of the novel that preceded this story), and the realization dawns simultaneously on the hero and the reader of the story alike that a casualty is imminent, that the young man, for all his style and charm, is on the verge of a fatal swing, that he is working without a net:

> His best suit he had sold for two dollars, but that was all right. He didn't mind at all about clothes. But the books. That was different. It made him very angry to think that there was no respect for men who wrote.
>
> He placed the shining penny on the table, looking upon it with the delight of a miser. How prettily it smiles, he said. Without reading them he looked at the words, *E Pluribus Unum One Cent United States Of America*, and turning the penny over, he saw Lincoln and the words, *In God We Trust Liberty 1923*. How beautiful it is, he said.
>
> He became drowsy and felt a ghastly illness coming over his blood, a feeling of nausea and disintegration. Bewildered, he stood beside his bed, thinking there *is nothing to do but sleep*. Already he felt himself making great strides through the fluid of the earth, swimming away to the beginning. He fell face down upon the bed, saying, I ought first at least to give the coin to some child. A child could buy any number of things with a penny.[6]

Implicit throughout the story is a vivid and rather cool-eyed awareness that America is an economy and not a culture. At the same time, the poetry of the story, its brilliant economy of means, ultimately accomplishes a kind of literary alchemy: it transcends the human tragedy of its theme, and in the end the reader is perhaps less moved by the narrative than impressed by the poise and daring of the young and—at the time this story appeared —unknown author.

This alchemy might be compared with the early freeze in Saroyan himself, which transformed and seemingly transcended an event of potentially devastating psychological consequences. Now, in the act of writing, he had transformed and seemingly transcended the tragedy implicit in a story, like Armenak's own, of a devastated and ultimately destroyed human life.

PERHAPS beyond anything else, the story was a triumph of style. For while its subject might be said to embody Armenak's side of Saroyan's nature, the manner of the writing itself has all the distancing and formal ingenuity that might be expected from that side of him, made literary and infinitely more sophisticated, for which Uncle Aram provided the closest prototype. Indeed, after having apparently made a quick but unerring assessment of all the available literary means at his disposal, from Joycean stream of consciousness to Hemingway's dictum of "grace under pressure," Saroyan, with one masterstroke, created here his own American-style amalgam: a streamlined, economy-sized, and immediately popular version of the best of innovative modern literature. And at the very center of this achievement is Saroyan's distinctive voice. Here is that voice as the world first knew it in the "WAKEFULNESS" part of the story:

> He (the living) dressed and shaved, grinning at himself in the mirror. Very unhandsome, he said; where is my tie? (He had but one.) Coffee and a gray sky, Pacific Ocean fog, the drone of a passing streetcar, people going to the city, time again, the day, prose and poetry. He moved swiftly down the stairs to the street and began to walk . . .[7]

The word "swift" would occur again and again in his writing from here on; and henceforth it would also be the personal trademark of Saroyan's method of composition. Having had this first story accepted by Whit Burnett and Martha Foley at *Story* magazine, Saroyan now proceeded to write a story a day for thirty successive days, and the results, published in *Story* and other magazines, eventually became his first book,

The Daring Young Man on the Flying Trapeze and Other Stories, published by Random House in September 1934.

I T is almost as if the twenty-six-year-old writer had arrived at the end of the long journey of his literary apprenticeship with a new kind of American product, "the Saroyan story," which he immediately set about mass producing and marketing as fast as he could, reaping the long-dreamed-of rewards of money and fame.

In this sense, the esthetic qualities of these stories are almost less interesting than the fact that an American literary artist had, it seemed, taken to heart the lessons of American industry and, in an unprecedented manner, applied them to his artistic practice. He became a phenomenon.

Having perceived America to be an economy rather than a genuine culture, Saroyan set about being an artist in a manner that might most deeply engage and interest a broad cross section of the population of such a society. He did not, either implicitly or explicitly, undertake an authentic critique of that society in the interests of making it more genuine and more human. Rather, he set about *demonstrating* the dynamics of the society in both his literary practice and his public persona, transforming them into his own myth. Like Hemingway before him, he became the literary equivalent of a movie star.

T H E R E is a distinction here that may be one of kind, rather than degree. At least this seems to be so in Saroyan's case. For even at the very highest level of his work, of which this first story is a justly famous example, Saroyan is essentially an *entertainer* first and foremost. He is out to please, often to move as well as to delight, but he will inevitably stop short of any real confrontation with the deepest implications of his own work. These implications, after all, would almost immediately lead him into levels of self-awareness, and consciousness of the political and social environment of self, that might seriously threaten his very character-structure—and perhaps even undermine the literary means he had found by which, at long last, he could liberate his life from its desolation and poverty.

The story that followed his debut in *Story* appeared in the April 1934 issue of the magazine and was called "Seventy Thousand Assyrians." It proved to be even more popular than its predecessor, to which the response had been unprecedented. In the first paragraph of this story,

*William Saroyan. 1934. This was perhaps Saroyan's favorite photograph of himself
as a young man. He considered the dour expression to be true to his deeper nature.*
(Photograph by Willard Van Dyke.)

written in the first person, can be seen perhaps even more clearly the nature of the gift he brought to his fellow Americans in the midst of their Depression years:

> I hadn't had a haircut in forty days and forty nights, and I was beginning to look like several violinists out of work. You know the look: genius gone to pot, and ready to join the Communist Party. We barbarians from Asia Minor are hairy people: when we need a haircut, we *need* a haircut. It was so bad, I had outgrown my only hat. (I am writing a very serious story, perhaps one of the most serious I shall ever write. That is why I am being flippant. Readers of Sherwood Anderson will begin to understand what I am saying after a while; they will know that my laughter is rather sad.) I was a young man in need of a haircut, so I went down to Third Street (San Francisco), to the Barber College, for a fifteen-cent haircut.[8]

The infectious gaiety of this story, as well as its genuinely touching moments, seemed to be just what the doctor ordered to lift the spirits of the ailing nation. These were days, remember, before television had pre-empted much of the impact of the written word, and *Story* magazine enjoyed a wide national readership. William Saroyan was now launched. It wasn't a question of the reading audience merely enjoying a new writer's work; it was very much as if people fell in love with this daring young man, who maintained such graceful high spirits in the face of their common adversity.

I T should probably be pointed out here that Saroyan, like any other entertainer, had his stock of tried and true effects, his own perennial bag of tricks, and from this celebrated beginning he set out graced with an unerring sense of just how to "play" his audience, to please and charm and move them, without ever genuinely probing or challenging his own—and, by extension, his readers'—deepest, least conscious, and most potent assumptions. It seems necessary to state this because it is sometimes hard not to confuse the effects of the entertainer with the fundamentally different purpose of the deeper artist, and in the case of William Saroyan, there was and probably continues to be confusion on this score.

. . .

THERE is, however, a third story that appeared in *The Daring Young Man on the Flying Trapeze*, which moves almost to its conclusion with the sustained promise of a revelation of the American psyche itself, and by extension the American world, only to stop short of its delivery and veer off into another dimension entirely. Perhaps because this story, called "Harry," makes the mistake of moving directly into territory from which it will ultimately retreat, it is one of the few stories in the book with a feeling of disappointment about it. Yet it is one of the most interesting stories in the collection, for it reveals the intersection, what seems to be the very fork in the road, where the entertainer and the deeper artist part company.

"This boy was a worldbeater,"[9] the story begins, and it goes on to delineate with the brilliant economy of Saroyan at his best the life and times of a great American salesman. Still in his teens, he is "to busy to fool around with girls."[10] In one of his earliest triumphs, he sells subscriptions to *True Stories* magazine door to door to immigrant housewives. Standing on the porch, holding up the magazine before a woman, he tells her: "Here is a lady ... who married a man thirty years older than her, and then fell in love with the man's sixteen year old son. Lady, what would *you* have done in such a fix?"[11] In the paragraph that follows, the consequences of his success swiftly unfold:

> In less than two months he had over sixty married women reading the magazine. Maybe he wasn't responsible, but after a while a lot of unconventional things began to happen. One or two wives had secret love affairs with other men and were found out by their husbands, who beat them or kicked them out of their houses, and a half dozen women began to send away for eye-lash beautifiers, bath salts, cold creams and things of that sort. The whole foreign neighborhood was getting to be slightly immoral. All the ladies began to rouge their lips and powder their faces and wear silk stockings and tight sweaters.[12]

The story goes on to show that Harry would sell virtually anything to anybody, and if it turned out that his customer wasn't able to pay for the electric refrigerator or the vacuum cleaner or the radio, Harry "would get five dollars down and a note for the balance, and if the man couldn't make his payments, Harry would attach the man's home, or his vineyard, or his automobile, or his horse, or anything else the man owned. And the amazing thing was that no one ever criticized him for his business methods. He was very smooth about attaching a man's property, and he would calmly explain that it was the usual procedure, according to law. What was right was right."[13]

Within the just discernible irony of the tone here, the human and social inner workings of the American way are being observed. More specifically, one is seeing the dynamic of a man somewhat on the order of Uncle Aram and of his impact on society at large. What is the fate of such a man? What is the fate of the society that creates him? These are the same fundamental questions asked by artists as different from one another as Theodore Dreiser and Charles Chaplin. In "Harry," Saroyan, too, is approaching a vision of his society.

Barely in his twenties, however, Harry becomes suddenly mortally ill, which seems at first to be begging the question; but then Saroyan has him trying to sell insurance to his cousin from his hospital bed, and one feels that maybe there hasn't been an artistic forfeiture here after all.

Then Harry dies, selling insurance straight to the end. But with his death, the author now completely abandons the implications and possible revelations of the story, as well as the lightly ironical tone, and concludes with three paragraphs of perhaps just slightly embarrassed ("the funniest stories about him are the ones that have to do with Harry in heaven, or in hell, selling earthquake insurance, and automobiles, and buying clothes cheap"[14]), but nonetheless outright, elegy. This is the final sentence of the story: "Everybody likes to laugh about him, but all the same this whole town misses him, and there isn't a man who knew him who doesn't wish that he was still among us, tearing around town, talking big business, making things pop, a real American go-getter."[15] One wonders, specifically, about those men who had their homes, or vineyards, or automobiles attached. Do they really miss Harry?

The young writer, having effectively forged his personality for the American literary marketplace and public of his day and being now in the first flush of worldly success after years of poverty and desolation, would

William Saroyan. 1936.

appear to be an apologist for the American Dream, even when he had promised to uncover its dark underside. "Harry" is actually no different in its essence than either of the other two stories, but perhaps it reveals this dimension more transparently.

3

FAME AND MONEY

FROM the moment of his success at the age of twenty-six, in 1934, to his induction into the army and his marriage soon after to the eighteen-year-old New York debutante Carol Marcus, in February 1943, lies the period of William Saroyan's most memorable work, as well as of his greatest adulation by the public.

The titles and dates of his collections of short stories during this period give some indication of the prodigious level of his literary production: *The Daring Young Man on the Flying Trapeze* (1934); *Inhale and Exhale* and *Three Times Three* (1936); *Little Children* (1937); *Love, Here Is My Hat* and *The Trouble with Tigers* (1938); *Peace, It's Wonderful* (1939); and *My Name Is Aram* (1940). Saroyan once estimated that he wrote some 500 tales during the first five years of his career.

William Saroyan and George Jean Nathan. New York. 1940.

Four portraits of Saroyan at the height of his fame.
(Photograph on facing page, lower right by Carl Van
Vechten.)

In addition to this work, beginning in 1939, he branched out into the American theater as well, with immediate, though controversial, success.* In April 1939, his play *My Heart's in the Highlands,* based on his own short story, opened on Broadway and was subsequently awarded the Drama Critics Circle Award for best play of the 1938–1939 season. And in October 1939, his play *The Time of Your Life* opened and eventually received both the Pulitzer Prize and the Drama Critics Circle Award for best play of the 1939–1940 season.

SAROYAN turned down the Pulitzer Prize, wiring the committee that had made the award that "commerce had no business patronizing art." This act caused a sensation, which, of course, created far more publicity than the award itself had.

There were most likely several motives behind Saroyan's rejection of the Pulitzer Prize, perhaps primary among them a feeling that at this high point of his career, the award, as well as its $1,000 honorarium, was unnecessary and irrelevant. When it would have made a difference, when he was sponging dimes off his brother each morning, the committee, along with everyone else, naturally couldn't have cared less. Now the award might even be said to bestow as much distinction on the Pulitzer name, by associating it with the names of already successful artists, as it did on the artists themselves. Who needed it?

There might have also been in this gesture a symbolic thumbing of his nose at Uncle Aram, the big success now long surpassed by his nephew Willie, whom Aram had once considered a bum. Saroyan loved to imitate his Uncle Aram, the great man, who was now being interviewed by reporters about his once lowly relative. Asked what his famous nephew was like in his early days, Aram once answered, with obvious impatience but, Saroyan seemed to feel, with amusing accuracy: "Willie . . . Willie was *nervous.*"

Finally, it seems possible that this award, generally considered America's highest literary honor, might have set off a kind of subterranean

* His first play had been written in 1935. Passing through New York, Saroyan had read in the *New York Times* that he was working on a play. To save the newspaper from error, he said, he immediately spent five days writing a play called "Subway Circus," which was never staged.

charge in the deeper reaches of Saroyan's emotional life: it might have touched him for just a moment at his frozen core. At thirty-two, the fatherless orphan was being given the official blessing of the establishment: the *national* fathers, so to speak, were showing him their favor and their love. If this award were construed in such a manner, even half consciously, and even for the briefest moment, it might have provided the strongest motive of all for his rejection of it. For it might threaten to melt his frozen center and unleash a profound emotional chaos.

It must also be added that Saroyan was most likely highly aware of the bonus in publicity that would attend his rejection of the award and that this would have in no sense deterred him—indeed, it most likely would have served as a positive incentive, perhaps even the primary, conscious one. From the beginning, he was a writer with a unique flair for publicity.

B U T accepting the possibility that one motive for his rejection of the Pulitzer Prize was that it threatened him psychologically, then there may be in this event the first overt indication of a psychological disability in Saroyan related to his earliest experience. It is interesting, too, that this would escape public scrutiny as such: that it would be thought of only as the maverick hijinks of a young and celebrated writer. No one would be likely to associate the rejection with a deeper psychological necessity. The act was, in this way, consistent with the writer's lifelong pattern of making his interior condition work to positive public effect, while more or less shunning any more intimate coming to terms with himself.

H O W E V E R, five years before the end of his life, Saroyan published a memoir, *Sons Come & Go, Mothers Hang in Forever*, in which he provides a vivid record of his official induction into this psychological pattern, which coincided with his separation from his mother at the orphanage. He speaks here, at sixty-seven, of an event that occurred before his third birthday, his first meeting with the superintendent of the Fred Finch Orphanage of Oakland:

> I met him in August of 1911, soon after Takoohi Saroyan had taken me to that place, and then in accordance with staff instructions had taken me to a small room in which to negotiate the separation.

The Fred Finch Orphanage, Central Building, Jacoby Hall. Oakland, California. 1911.

BELOW AND RIGHT: *The earliest admission date for the Saroyan children that is available in Fred Finch Orphanage records is March 16, 1912. The four children appear to have been discharged from the orphanage for the summer of 1913. They were then readmitted on September 10, 1913, and discharged for the final time on June 15, 1916. The crossing out of the original admission date may reflect the fact that the four children were admitted to the orphanage after being discharged for the summer of 1913.*

Cozette SAROYAN- Turkey PLACE of Birth - DATE Birth
came 14 Jan 22 - 1899
Zabel   " (Home) "   11 apr 11 - 1902
Henry   " (State) "   8. aug 3 - 1905
William " (State) Fresno 5 aug 13 - 1908

all left the Home in 1916 to live with
mother at Fresno
The records show Home received only
12.50 per month for care of the four children
Henry and William being on state aid
at 6.25 each per month as state then
paid only 75 per year per child.

BACKGROUND: *Younger children and staff at Fred Finch Orphanage. Early 1900s.*

Name William Saroyan No. 1333 No. _____
Place of birth Fresno, Cali.
Date of birth Aug. 13, 1908 Age when admitted 3 yr. 8
Date of admission Mar. 15, 12 Date of discharge _____
Estate or Insurance None
Place where parents died Father, Campbell, Calif.
Nativity of father Armenian Mother Armenian
Where married Bitlis, Turkey in Asia.
Marriage Certificate recorded Bitlis, Asia.
Character of parents Fine
Came to California 1907
Name who pays No one pays the Mother is poor
Address _____

HALF ORPHANS Admitted 9-15-1913 HISTORY CARD FOR CHILDREN'S INSTITUTIONS No. 7

Name of Institution Fred Finch Orphanage Dism 6-15 1916
Name of Child Saroyan, William Place of Birth Fresno, Cal Date of Birth Aug. 13, 1908
Name of Person Responsible for Child Mrs. T.A. Saroyan {Mother, Father, Guardian, Other.
Address Fresno, California 239 N Street

NAME	Birth Date	Date of Death	Nativity	Religion	Date of Naturalization	Occupation	Income	Physical or Mental Defects	Marital Condition		Public Charges	
F. Armenag Saroyan		7/19/11	Armenian	Presbyt		minister			* MC. Div. Des. Sep. Wid. Widr. UMC. UM. RM.	F. Insane State County M. Insane State County F. Jailed State County M. Jailed State County		
M. Takoohi Saroyan			Armenian									

NAME OF CHILD	Date of Admission	Form of Admission.	Board Paid By	Amount	Property or Insurance
William Saroyan	Sept 10, 1913	Committed by Juvenile Court; (a) Needy. (b) Wayward. Transferred from other institution. Parent or guardian. ✓	State. County. Mother. Father. Guardian. Others. ✓	$.25 mo.	none

HEIGHT		WEIGHT		**Disease	Physical or Mental Defects	SCHOOL GRADE		VOCATIONAL TRAINING	
At Entrance	At Dismissal	At Entrance	At Dismissal			At Entrance May 1916	At Dismissal	At Entrance	At Dismissal
							2		

(Indicate by check in column.)
DISPOSITION — REASON: — PERSON OR INSTITUTION TO WHOM DISMISSED***

✓ Returned to parent or guardian.
Placed in free home.
Placed for service.
Transferred to child-placing agency.
Adopted.

Left without permission.
Transferred to Juvenile Court.
Sent to hospital.
Recovered.
Died.
Dismissed from hospital to parent.

PLACEMENTS	DATE	NAME	ADDRESS
First	6/15/16	Mrs T Saroyan	Fresno Cal
Returned			
Replaced			

*The above abbreviations mean: MC. Married Couple; Div. Divorce; Des. Deserted; Sep. Separated; Wid. Widow; Widr. Widower; UMC. Unmarried Couple; UM. Unmarried Mother; RM. Re-married.
**Record here all serious illness with date and duration.
(over)
***On back of this card or on separate card, "Alumni card", keep a record of the child's history after leaving the institution.

State Board of Charities and Corrections—1914. California
A. CARLISLE & CO., 251 BUSH ST., S. F.

I began to cry and she said, "No, you are a man now, and men do not cry." So I stopped crying.

She gave me a mechanical toy which was named *The Coon Jigger*. Wind him up and he danced, himself all tin, dancing madly on a tin stage. Once was enough, though.

I was then alone in the small room that I still remember as having smelled deathly as well as oily from some kind of stupid furniture polish, for what could possibly be more stupid to a small boy under such circumstances than the polishing of dismal institutional furniture?

After I had been alone long enough to go over my whole future life, perhaps several times, after surely not more than three or four very quiet minutes, the door from the main office opened and in came this man who seemed very big and very old.

The man was Mr. Hagen, as he was called, and he was surely not more than six feet tall, not heavy at all, and not more than forty years of age.

"Well, now," he said, "let's go right on being sensible this way."[1]

That he found it possible, at so young an age, to behave in so stalwart a manner seems to have surprised even Mr. Hagen—and Saroyan would go on to make this capacity to surprise and even astonish people a lifelong habit. But to watch this small boy, only barely out of infancy, swallow his tears and stop crying before his mother leaves the room, is also to witness a scene of the most fundamental physical and psychological re-orientation of energy, and a subsequent human transformation. In effect, the energy that wants to issue itself as grief begins to do so and then is summarily dismissed by Takoohi, so that it is forced to redirect itself into stopping the grief. And this course of interior action is then rewarded by Mr. Hagen's remark that this is the sensible way in which to behave.

This is the interior mechanism of the freeze itself, given immediate support and vindication by the orphan's surrogate parent. The grief that wasn't released here in the process of redirecting its energy to check the tears might now be said to be contained in the body more or less "on ice."

·   ·   ·

I T may also be possible that this suppression of grief by the power of his will—initiated at the orphanage and then presumably sustained through Saroyan's five years there—created that habit of extraordinary self-discipline which in the grown man would produce an enormous quantity of literature, a great deal of it written with unprecedented speed.

There are clear indications that as a writer Saroyan positively enjoyed the pressure of a self-imposed deadline—from his first book, written a story a day in thirty days, to his most celebrated feat of accelerated creativity, the writing of *The Time of Your Life* in six days at the Great Northern Hotel in New York.

In the novel *One Day in the Afternoon of the World,* published in 1964, Saroyan has his alter ego, a writer in his late forties named Yep Muscat, speak of this personal method of playwriting to an aspiring Broadway producer. Asked how long it took him to write his most famous play, he answers:

> "Six days. As a matter of fact, once I get started, I try to finish every new play in six days . . . writing has very little to do with speed, or time. It's pretty much a matter of concentration. If one playwright takes a year to write a new play and another takes a week, they've both concentrated about the same amount—enough to write a new play. I get bored quickly, so I can't have an unfinished play badgering me for very long."[2]

Whatever the genre, Saroyan apparently always worked against a deadline. He would give himself two months, for example, to write a novel or a memoir, and he might even allow the daily installments to determine the form. The deadlines seem to have functioned to organize his time, to provide him with a working schedule which, once he had honored it, would also give him daily free time. He would often pursue two (or more) projects this way simultaneously, working on one in the morning and the other in the afternoon. This procedure also answered what appears to have been for Saroyan a real need to know that he had *some* writing around to do on a daily basis almost all the time.

A T the beginning of his career, the short story form satisfied this need and supplied him with a daily commercial product at the same time. In the dedications to the two collections of stories that Saroyan published in 1938, *Love, Here Is My Hat* and *The Trouble with Tigers*, one gets a vivid sense of his delight in being able to produce in the form of a book an article of contemporary merchandise, simultaneously satisfying the entirely different sides of his psychological being, the one born of Armenak, the other of Uncle Aram. Here is the dedication to *The Trouble with Tigers*:

> This book is for the one who opens it. The gambler who comes here for whatever he may find here, wagering his time and boredom against my talent and eagerness. The idler with a couple more hours to kill. The eager one who seeks in the printed page the answer to whatever question is troubling him most at the time. The bad writer who is grateful for good writing. The good writer who knows that good contemporaries make him better. The unpublished writer who wants to find out how it's done. The critic who is sick of print. The ladies and gentlemen who read to be in style. The explorer in the hush of the Public Library. I accept all challengers, the worthy and the unworthy. What I want to do is please you, whoever you are and whatever brings you here. If you find a page that is not what you think it should be, tear it out and throw it away. Forgive me if I bore you; for if I bore you, I forgive you. Happy book, please the ladies and take care of my fame.[3]

Love, Here Is My Hat, one of the first books and still among the few by a celebrated American writer to be published as a "paperback original," is dedicated as follows by the author to his publisher:

> This book is dedicated with affection and admiration to Modern Age Books, Inc., for encouraging the romance between life and letters by reducing the fee per affair from $2.50 to 25¢, without making a whore of the lady.[4]

This is Saroyan in his heyday: the handsome, iconoclastic, devil-may-care, American genius, delighting in his talent, his fame, and his luck.

He had found the means now by which to turn an inner necessity to write—employing perhaps the same psychic mechanism that he had used to contain his unreleased and immobilized grief and that had earlier caused him to place such emphasis on physical mobility and speed—into an artistic, but nonetheless commercial, American product, bringing with it the immediate rewards of money and fame.

H E was now a literary hero in America, but nowhere more so than in San Francisco, where he lived. He bought his mother a house at the top of the Sunset District and had a bedroom-studio built downstairs for himself. He went out with the tennis star, Helen Wills Moody. He made the night life in San Francisco jump with his loud voice and deep laughter, his stories and jokes, his bravura and charm. Walking into Vanessi's one night in North Beach, he saw a young and lovely woman seated alone at the bar. Urged on by his admiration and delight, he smiled at the perfect stranger, sauntered over to her, and kissed her on the mouth. She, in turn, met and returned his kiss.

Once he was invited to dinner by an attractive woman he had met at a party with her husband. When he arrived at the couple's house, the woman answered the door wearing little more than a smile, and invited him in. The husband, it seemed, had been called away at the last minute. Even so, this was a little more than Saroyan had bargained for, and although he found the woman attractive, he found himself momentarily disinclined.

He was also a frequenter of San Francisco's houses of prostitution, as readers of his early stories know, and became familiar enough with them to know many of the girls, as well as the madams, by name. In several of the stories, he speaks of an impulse to rescue one or another of the young women, but in his life no such impulse was ever to be carried through.

A N O T H E R important dimension of the early Saroyan persona, and one frequently referred to in the early stories, is his interest in most of the popular varieties of gambling, notably horse racing and card games, but also, though less frequently, the casino-style games of roulette and baccarat. Saroyan himself admitted that he wasn't a careful gambler, and even on occasion seemed to suggest that any such order of gambler was a contradiction in terms. Winning at gambling for him meant luck, as opposed to skill. Although in his later years he would come to admire the abilities of the fine poker player, for example, he himself was uninterested or simply temperamentally incapable of this application of discipline. It seems likely that after his success, gambling became something of an "escape valve" for him after the daily rigors of writing. From the outset, winning seems to have been at best a secondary objective. The real point was to gamble with such all-out daring that it would perhaps even "court" luck.

This approach to gambling embodies a kind of symbolic parallel to Saroyan's approach to his art. For in each story he wrote, he eschewed all pat formulas and went on his nerve. As often as not, he seemed to build his tales musically, riding an inner rhythm, holding onto it all the way through, like a good luck charm. If he was lucky, in two or three hours' time he found he had completed a brand-new story. And if he missed—if the story didn't quite work all the way through, seeming in the end a bit fragmentary, more of a sketch than a real story, it was nevertheless imbued with the Saroyan touch, that jazzlike improvisatory manner that was the real mark of his genius. And he would carry this boldness so far as to publish virtually all of these early tales as well.

IN terms of literary quality, however, after *The Daring Young Man on the Flying Trapeze* there is a falling off in the excitement, the interior compression and momentum, of the individual stories, until *My Name Is Aram*, which collects stories written in 1937, 1938, 1939, and 1940, all of which are lyrical and rather idealized memoirs of Saroyan's Fresno childhood. This book, unified by the elegiac mood with which the adult writer looks back on his childhood, is, story for story, Saroyan's finest collection—a wonderfully sustained paean to the life he knew as a child among the Armenian immigrants and their children in the San Joaquin Valley. In such stories as "The Summer of the Beautiful White Horse," "The Three Swimmers and the Grocer from Yale," and "The Pomegranate Trees," Saroyan's quality of innocence, his disinclination to look directly into the darker dimensions of his own experience, has found a near perfect subject. For if life is ever truly like a fairy tale, it is most likely at just that moment of childhood that this book so lovingly captures. This is the opening of the book's first story, "The Summer of the Beautiful White Horse":

One day back there in the good old days when I was nine and the world was full of every imaginable kind of magnificence, and life was still a delightful and mysterious dream, my cousin Mourad, who was considered crazy by everybody who knew him except me, came to my house at four in the morning and woke me up by tapping on the window of my room.

Aram, he said.

I jumped out of bed and looked out the window.

I couldn't believe what I saw.

It wasn't morning yet, but it was summer and with daybreak not many minutes around the corner of the world it was light enough for me to know I wasn't dreaming.

My cousin Mourad was sitting on a beautiful white horse.[5]

SIMILARLY, Saroyan's most famous play, *The Time of Your Life*, weaves an almost palpable spell over the stage, although in retrospect it may be seen to have far less substance than at first appeared to be the case. But the style here is a revelation of Saroyan's particular magic as an artist, and perhaps it is easier to observe it objectively on the stage than on the printed page.

The Time of Your Life is, in a way, a celebration of physical mobility that often borders on outright choreography. The play is dominated less by characters with any genuine claim on our attention than by a pervasive dancelike momentum that moves from one area of the stage to another among random habitués of a San Francisco waterfront saloon, never settling long enough on any one of them to catch more than a kind of mythological glimpse of character but sweeping us up in its movement, much as we are swept up in the stylistic exuberance of Saroyan's best prose.

This is writing—or playwrighting—that continually verges on music, and, like many of the best popular songs that infect one with a literally physical delight, the verbal content is secondary. The essential thing is the movement, the rhythm, the melodic play of the piece, and Saroyan at his best had an intuitive mastery of this dimension.

In 1948, James Agee, a close contemporary of Saroyan's, reviewed the film version of *The Time of Your Life* in *Time* magazine, and in this review gave as clear-eyed and evenhanded an assessment of his work as Saroyan was to receive in his lifetime. Nevertheless, one senses in Agee the fundamental distrust and impatience of an artist of an entirely different order with the undeniable yet suspect effectiveness of an enviably successful peer:

Saroyan is an entertainer of a kind overrated by some people and underrated by others—a very gifted schmalz-artist. In the schmalz-artist strength and weakness are inextricably combined—the deeply, primordially valid, and the falseness of the middle-aged little boy who dives back into the womb for pennies.

The schmalz-artist requires more belief, more wishful thinking on the part of his audience, than better artists would dare require. Reality is as much his deadly enemy as it is the superior artist's most difficult love affair. At his best, Saroyan is a wonderfully sweet-natured, witty and beguiling kind of Christian anarchist, and so apt a lyrical magician that the magic designed for one medium still works in another. At his worst, he is one of the world's ranking contenders for brassy, self-pitying, arty mawkishness, for idealism with an eye to the main chance, for arrogant determination to tell damnably silly lies in the teeth of truth.

Except in Saroyan's world, barroom philosophers who intrude on new customers with the words "What's the dream?" are seldom answered courteously; and when euphoria enchants any saloon for more than five consecutive minutes, you can expect a quick return of trouble, or boredom, or both. The face on Saroyan's barroom floor has something unassailably good about the eyes. But the smile is that of a swindling parson who is sure his own swindle is for the greater glory of God.[6]

The difficulty Saroyan had in bringing forward and convincingly embodying in his writing the darker side of human reality is at the heart of his artistic identity. It was a fundamental part of his appeal during the Depression-torn days of his greatest fame. But at the same time, even at the beginning, it prevented him from access to human experience in all its complexity that is the mark of the deeper artist.

One might even explain the high quality of the stories published in *The Daring Young Man on the Flying Trapeze*, despite the limitations noted, by observing that they were written at a time when Saroyan's life circumstances reinforced the darker aspects of reality; hence the stories have a quality of wholeness about them, a feeling for the grit and detail of actual life, that was seldom to be so fully apparent in his writing again.

For success, strong and swift when it came, delivered him almost entirely out of the circumstances that had given the impetus and emotional background for those first stories. Now he was unable to lay claim to that dark side by means of the poverty and desolation he had known as a struggling young writer. Henceforth, he would almost inevitably be denied access to it.

Gertrude Stein once observed that "American success is American failure," and the enigmatic truth of this statement may be glimpsed in what seems to have been Saroyan's more or less unconscious struggle to reclaim the creative wellspring he had known when his back had been to the wall.

Gambling, then, might have been one of the primary means by which he tried to renew his acquaintance with the dark side of experience. For although he could be sensible about money, wasting no time in setting up his mother and himself in a new home, there is no question that Saroyan threw away a small fortune during the period of his greatest success. In his novel *Boys and Girls Together*, published in 1963, his alter ego, a writer named Charley, at one point estimates he had thrown away about $250,000 gambling during the days preceding his marriage (obviously a far more significant sum in those Depression years than in the 1980s). He had, in fact, a reputation for being a wild man as a gambler, and this reputation doesn't seem to have been unwarranted.

IT is possible to surmise from this that Saroyan was throwing his money where he may have found it impossible to venture his own person, that he was symbolically delving into the darkness with his dollars in lieu of exploring his own deeper emotional life. The gambler plunges his money into the unknown, in effect surrendering a financial surrogate of himself to the winds of chance. If he wins, he has been smiled upon by the gods. But if he loses, he will feel the pinch in his own earthly shoes. Losing, therefore, might have been one way the young writer could again experience at least something of the pain and darkness he had known in the days before fame and money removed him into another world.

There is a possibility, then, that a kind of spiritual and psychological amputation attended Saroyan's success—though in essence that had already occurred in his habitual denial of grief while in the orphanage. Compulsive gambling may have been the more or less unconscious attempt to undo the damage. From early childhood, he had learned to contain his grief by inner discipline, harnessing the energy of grief in the attempt to thwart it. And, perhaps, even his writing was only the latest manifestation of this harnessed, metamorphosed energy of his being. But as an artist, it would be difficult, if not impossible, for him to reveal and illuminate life once success removed him from experiencing any form of grief, error, desperation, or any other dimension of the underside, the night side, of human experience.

4

AT LONG LAST LOVE

CAROL MARCUS was just seventeen when she met William Saroyan. He was thirty-four—and riding high on the crest of his fame.

She was blond and beautiful, witty, and innocent but daring. She had recently graduated from Dalton School in Manhattan, and she had played a small role in a production of Saroyan's play *Jim Dandy*, having been suggested for the part by a young friend, at Princeton. Her two best friends were Oona O'Neill and Gloria Vanderbilt. She happened to be in Los Angeles in February 1942 because she had come out to be the bridesmaid at Gloria's wedding to the agent Pat di Cicco.

Saroyan was in Los Angeles because he had written a screenplay called "The Human Comedy" (the precursor of the novel) that he wanted to sell to Metro Goldwyn Mayer and that they wanted to buy from him.

The celebrated writer from San Francisco and the beautiful young debutante from New York's Park Avenue were introduced one night at a Hollywood restaurant by a mutual friend, the musician and bandleader, Artie Shaw.

GIVEN Saroyan's psychological character, the basic question is whether for him at this point love was a possibility; whether it was even desirable. Leaving aside for the moment the hypothesized interior freeze, he would seem generally to have had the tendencies of an obsessive-compulsive character type, a type not uncommon among artists and others especially preoccupied with their work.

Harry Stack Sullivan, the pioneering American psychiatrist, characterized this obsessive mechanism as frequently acting as a "screen" for deeper, highly charged but unresolved emotion that remains unconscious—and this seems to be a more or less accurate description of Saroyan's case. It doesn't seem unlikely that the experience of falling in love might cause conflict in this type of personality.

SAROYAN and Carol Marcus were married and divorced twice in eight years, indicative in itself of the ambivalence implicit in their relationship. Perhaps Saroyan's clearest statement of his own feelings at the beginning of the relationship occurs in a passage of his novel, *Boys and Girls Together*, published in 1963 but most likely written in the late 1940s or early 1950s. The scene described here, or at least a variation on it, actually occurred. It took place in the Hampshire House hotel on Central Park South, where Saroyan had rented a suite while producing and directing his two one-act plays, *Across the Board on Tomorrow Morning* and *Talking to You*, in the fall of 1942. The plays were staged at the Saroyan Theater, as he had rechristened the Belasco on Broadway; and the producer-director-writer had given both Carol and her friend Oona O'Neill small parts in the production.

The plays had opened to bad reviews, and at the same time Saroyan received his draft notice. After not hearing from him for several days, Carol, with whom he had now initiated an affair—the first of her life—had gone to see him at his Hampshire House suite. The passage in the novel recalls the scene inside a narrative that occurs seven years later:

Carol. New York. 1944. (Photograph by G. Maillard Kesslere.)

The woman began to cry again, only this time is was the big beautiful baby bawling, bawling the way she had bawled when he had told her so long ago in New York to go home and not bother herself about him any more, told her he had work to do, told her to go back to the boys who didn't have work to do, and she went, but an hour later when he stepped out of his apartment to take a walk and pick up the morning papers, there she was sitting on the marble bench just outside his door bawling and blubbering, her eyes red, her face red, her mouth wet with slobber, and he thought, Have I got this whole thing wrong? Is it possible that this girl is so much more than she seems to be? Am I so stupid as not to have found out anything about her at all after all this time?

"I was going to go in a minute," she wept. "I was just going to go."

"What are you crying about?"

"I don't know. I don't know, but I wish you knew how it is."

Is it possible? he thought. I've treated her the way I believed she deserved to be treated, like a vagrant piece. What the devil is this?

"Well, come back in here and wash your face. Then I'll walk you home if that's where you want to go."

"I don't want to go home," she wept. "I never want to go home again. I want to stay here the rest of my life."

"This apartment's twenty-five dollars a day, I'm leaving it in a few days to go into the Army."

"I want to go with you," she wept, only she wasn't trying to be funny, she was just sick, he couldn't imagine how she could have ever gotten so sick. He could imagine her getting sick of him as he had gotten sick of her—until now—until this incredible unbelievable bawling that was impossible to disbelieve, for nothing seemed to stop it, not even cold water splashed on her face. What the devil was she bawling *about*?

And why had she picked him to hear it? All he had wanted was another piece, a better one than most for being younger and prettier and funnier, so what was all the bawling about?[1]

It seems clear that it was about love, for Carol a very powerful first love, and making allowances for the inevitable distortions in the transfor-

mation of experience into novel form, it is remarkable to see the dynamics
of this relationship from Saroyan's point of view. For one thing, he apparently found the young woman's revelation of her feelings a complete surprise. He seems to have been stunned by her emotion, her grief. And yet, at
the same time, witnessing it first hand in this way seems almost immediately to have catalyzed his own feelings:

> He could imagine her getting sick of him as he had gotten sick of her—
> *until now* [italics mine]—until this incredible unbelievable bawling
> that was impossible to disbelieve, for nothing seemed to stop it, . . .[2]

Suddenly, he finds himself face to face with someone who is obviously
deeply in love with him, someone he says he himself had grown sick of,
had never taken seriously in the first place. But the implication is that he is
profoundly changed by what he has now seen: "he had gotten sick of
her—until now—until this incredible unbelievable bawling *that was impossible to disbelieve* [italics mine], . . ."[3] The implication here is that he
previously distrusted the authenticity of her feelings—or perhaps this distrust is more fundamental, more generalized, directed not just at her but at
all women. He seems to be *convinced* by her crying. It dispels his doubts,
so that almost instantaneously their relationship has real significance for
him, whereas before it appears to have meant nothing to him at all.

W H A T seems to have been a certain insensitivity in Saroyan, more or less
self-confessed in the passage quoted, may indeed be, at least in part, a
product of a general suspicion of women, one reflecting his experience
of women in childhood. In the first place, there is the whole question of his
mother's role in Armenak's death. The ambiguity here, regardless of the
objective truth of the matter—most likely irretrievable—would be enough
to make Saroyan uneasy. On top of this, there is Takoohi's notably callous
treatment of her youngest child at their separation at the orphanage,
though interestingly enough, in recalling this episode in the memoir
quoted earlier, Saroyan does not comment on it. Or, later, her scorn for his
indulgence in an afternoon baseball game. Finally, family lore has it that
Takoohi would sometimes beat her son with a broom, and that when she
put her children in the tub for a bath, she would scrub them till their

skin was red and chafed. In summary, she must have been a tough and forbidding woman at the very least and perhaps one with an edge of outright menace about her.

BEYOND Takoohi, there were Saroyan's two older sisters, the women teachers and the girls in his classes at school, and, finally and perhaps most importantly, the prostitutes he got to know through his job as a Postal Telegraph messenger in Fresno. From his report, these women were attractive and always had a casual, kind word for the adolescent messenger, as well as generous tips. But they were considered "bad" women, morally objectionable by the standards of the community at large.

However, the so-called "good" women, especially within the Armenian immigrant community itself, were for the most part housewives, mothers, or older sisters, whose role was centered in, if not almost confined to, the kitchen: a role that vividly contrasts with and is in its way just as limiting as the bedroom role to which the prostitutes were primarily confined.

This dichotomy between "good" and "bad" women—between those in the kitchen and those in the bedroom—seems to have plagued Saroyan, confusing and stunting his relationships with women all his life. After the failure of his marriages to Carol, he appears never again to have had even a single serious affair. He went to prostitutes instead, where the terms of the relationship were defined financially, rather than emotionally. He seems to have felt that this was the most comfortable arrangement. In the end, however, this "solution" looks very much like an interior expediency that ultimately would bar access to deeper levels of experience in the same way as his freezing of his grief had done. Indeed, it may be that this first, involuntary reaction set the pattern for what was to become a psychological habit.

IN witnessing Carol's grief outside his Hampshire House suite, however, he apparently experienced a deeper sense of the autonomous identity of a woman and, at the same time, a deeper sense of a human, as opposed to an exclusively sexual, connection between another and himself, than he had ever known before. The paradox here, of course, is that the act that triggered this moment of deeper involvement was a display of helpless tears, that very grief that he himself had been forbidden by Takoohi to show when they separated at the orphanage—and which by the force of his will he had apparently redirected, rechanneled, until he scarcely seemed conscious of its existence at all.

But now this same order of grief, witnessed in a young woman, immediately banished all previous doubts he had about her authenticity. He knew that it was real! In spite of his own internal prohibition of grief, he recognized this grief as if it was a kind of human absolute. The fact that she was crying and could not stop crying was seemingly all that he needed to know about her: and perhaps it was the *only* thing that could ever have convinced him that she was genuine.

T H E R E is no question that this was an authentic moment of human recognition in Saroyan's life. It marked an immediate deepening in his relationship with Carol, resulting ultimately in their marriage. At the same time, he seems to have had a flash of insight in response to Carol's intense emotional experience. Her grief became real enough to him for him to see her, apparently for the first time, in a way that acknowledged her own complexity as a person. And yet, such a moment of insight would almost of necessity conflict with Saroyan's habit of repressing and, as it were, psychically reconditioning his own deepest emotional reality. He would almost necessarily have to be shocked into acknowledging in another person what he had now spent close to half a lifetime not acknowledging in himself.

5

BILL AND CAROL

SAROYAN once said, in explaining his involvement with Carol, that he
had fallen in love with her past. He made the remark years after the period
of their two marriages and divorces, and it has a quality of sober insight
that is uncharacteristic of the writer's usual, off-the-top conversational
style. It suggests an uncommon depth of thought and feeling.

IN her own way, Carol was as unlikely a New York debutante as Bill, after
the pain and deprivation of his youth, was a world-famous American
writer.

Carol's mother, whose maiden name was Rosheen Brophman and
whose family were Jewish immigrants from a rural area near Kiev, Russia,
was a beautiful, headstrong girl of sixteen. Her family was outraged by

a love affair she was having at age sixteen and threw her out of their apartment on Gramercy Park in Manhattan. She gave birth to a daughter, Carol, on September 11, 1924, but, too poor to care for her, she was forced to put the baby in foster homes so that she could go to work. Rosheen visited the little girl whenever she could manage. And she was a loving mother when she was with her daughter. But it was always necessary to leave—and the child would be left once again to the strangers with whom she had been boarded.

T H E N Rosheen's family arranged for her to be married to an older man named Shepherd, a New York University philosophy teacher, and Rosheen brought Carol home to live with her and her new husband. Soon the couple had a child of their own, a daughter they named Elinor. However, the evening Rosheen brought her new daughter home from the hospital, while she and her husband were bathing the baby, Shepherd, who apparently had never taken kindly to little Carol, remarked to his wife that now that they had their own child, the two-year-old girl in the corner of the room could be put up for adoption.

Rosheen's character, her maternal commitment and protectiveness despite all difficulties, is vividly underscored by her response to her husband's remark. She ceased giving Elinor a bath, left her to the care of her father, threw a coat over Carol and one over herself, and walked out of her husband's New York apartment with her older daughter, never to return.

T H E R E now followed another period of foster homes for both of Rosheen's daughters, since Shepherd apparently was either unable or unwilling to care for Elinor himself. Eventually, both little girls found more or less permanent foster parents.

Before finding such a home, however, Carol felt mostly like an unwanted guest in the homes of the families, often large and close to poverty themselves, that took her in. She was often forced to share a bed with others, and in an effort to be less conspicuous would make herself as small and hold herself as still as she could.

At meals, she felt that food was hers only after it had gone the rounds of the family proper, and she would sometimes go hungry as a result. Once, at the end of a meal, she was eyeing a leftover piece of bacon, only to have it snatched up by an older boy in the house who told her, "This is for me—not you!"

The fragility of the child's state of mind at this time can be observed in one of her earliest experiences in the home of her final foster parent, a Catholic woman named Genevieve Laragay, who lived in Paterson, New Jersey. Carol had arrived on Christmas Eve, and although she was taken to her room that first evening without being allowed to explore the rest of the house, she nevertheless caught a glimpse of a large and beautiful Christmas tree, which filled her with excitement and awe.

On Christmas day, she was allowed to feast her eyes on the whole tree, and she was even given a present of her own from under it. When Rosheen called later in the day to ask how she was, Carol told her everything was wonderful, and this unusual response may have convinced Rosheen to board her daughter permanently with Genevieve. From that first day, the child loved to sit in the living room contemplating the tree.

Then one morning when Carol came downstairs for breakfast, the tree was gone. The little girl was thrown into a grief-stricken panic. Where had the tree gone? How could it just disappear like that? Genevieve attempted to explain to her that it was a Christmas tree and that there would be another one next year just like it. But the four-year-old child was inconsolable. She had believed the tree was a unique feature of the house—that it somehow had grown in the living room.

When every attempt Genevieve made to soothe her had failed, she finally told Carol that she must stop crying and that if she did, she would allow her to engage in a pastime she loved perhaps only a little less than sitting with the tree: brushing Genevieve's long hair. This calmed Carol somewhat. She took the brush, Genevieve undid her long tresses, and the little girl began to brush. But then, abruptly, she couldn't go on. Suddenly, she was seized with a fear that if she kept on brushing, Genevieve's head would fall off and roll away and be gone like the Christmas tree.

Eventually, Carol was able to settle down with Genevieve for several years of care and relative happiness, with periodic visits—emotional and inevitably disheartening because they were only visits—from her mother, Rosheen.

.   .   .

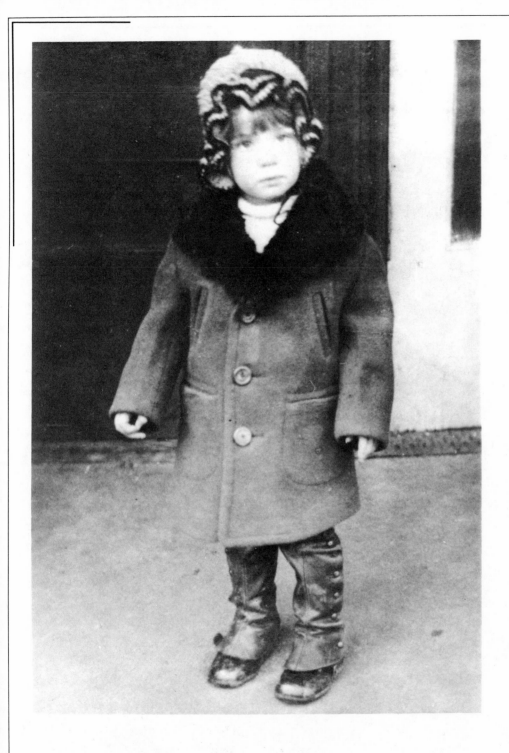

Carol Marcus as an orphan. c. 1926. Saroyan was moved by the way the little girl held her right hand with finger and thumb touching.

FAR LEFT: *Rosheen. c. 1931.*

LEFT: *Charles Marcus.*

BELOW: *Carol and Oona O'Neill. Los Angeles. 1947.*

.   .   .

T H E N something extraordinary happened. One day Rosheen called for her daughter and brought her into New York to a new apartment she had in the West Seventies. It was larger than any of Rosheen's earlier apartments, and it was handsomely furnished. Rosheen herself was dressed in beautiful new clothes and seemed happier than she had been for a long time.

As a veteran of foster homes, Carol had developed a self-protective ability to melt into the background among strangers, and that is what she did when, later that afternoon, mother and daughter were visited by a man named Charles Marcus, a scientist and vice president of Bendix Aviation.

As the tall and distinguished-looking man sat in the living room of the apartment that he had rented for Rosheen, who at the moment was getting drinks in the kitchen, young Carol stood watching him from behind a chair. In her hand, she held an ancient bean bag, a favorite toy she liked to carry with her everywhere. As she watched the man, it seemed to her that he might have been smiling at her, although in the room's suffused light she couldn't be sure.

Suddenly, the little girl, almost *certain* now that the man was smiling at her, took heart and, with uncharacteristic courage, acted on impulse. She took a step from behind the chair that had been shielding her, looked the stranger directly in the eye, and flung her beanbag at him with all her might.

Charles Marcus caught it. Then he threw it back to her.

Carol, in turn, caught it.

"Well," the man said, delighted, "you're a good catch."

That afternoon, Charles Marcus took Rosheen and Carol out for tea. He cared for the little girl, apparently, as much as he cared for her mother. A short time later, he married Rosheen and henceforth she and her daughter lived with him in a large apartment on Park Avenue. Along with Rosheen, Carol now took the name Marcus. It remained for Rosheen to tell her husband of her other daughter, and she was only able to bring herself to do this after several years, whereupon Charles Marcus had Elinor join their family as well.

F R O M the age of eight, Carol lived the life of an upper-class New York girl. She proved to be a good student at Dalton. Having attended a performance of *The Time of Your Life* on Broadway, Carol considered writing about the controversial (and handsome!) young playwright, William Saroyan, for her senior paper at Dalton, but she eventually decided to write about T. S. Eliot instead. Her intellectual side was nurtured by her contact with Charles Marcus, who cared about the young girl as if she were his own daughter.

Along with her friends Gloria and Oona, she was considered among the most sought-after of New York debutantes. She dated, among others, Kingdon Gould, scion of the wealthy New York family, and Stevie Hopkins, the son of Harry Hopkins, Franklin Delano Roosevelt's advisor and aide. She and Oona also both worked as actresses in summer theater. After her graduation, a beau of Gloria's named Geoffry Jones invited Carol to Princeton to play a role in a new Saroyan play, *Jim Dandy*, which Jones also was to play a part in.

SAROYAN discovered the details of Carol's early life only after he had married her, and at first he was angered that this information—which contradicted the public assumptions about his wife's past—had been withheld from him. In fact, the revelation of one aspect of his wife's background seems to have been the major motivation for the couple's first divorce. More than anything else, the discovery that his wife was Jewish disturbed Saroyan. On one occasion before they were married, when the writer and a number of other Armenians had been speaking deprecatingly of Jews—more or less a commonplace among Armenians of Saroyan's generation—Carol, in momentary social embarrassment bordering on fright, had reflexively denied that she was Jewish. Nevertheless, as his later remark about falling in love with her past attests, at a certain point Bill came to value Carol's early history, and perhaps even to identify with it.

FOR these two people, so different in age, character, and temperament, shared from their early childhoods an intimate knowledge of the darker byways of the American experience. Each had been an orphan. Though in different ways, each seems to have had a public veneer that combined charm and bravura—a kind of social charisma—and each seems to have known a corresponding private insecurity.

Both, too, came from minorities that were still unassimilated in the American world. Saroyan had known prejudice against Armenians at first hand in his childhood: "For Sale" signs posted in front of houses with "No Armenians" written beneath in smaller letters; a grammar school teacher who complained to the class of the odor of spicy food on the Armenian children's breath. Carol, however, had come of age in an upper-class, eastern-seaboard social milieu in which there was no blatant prejudice.

The way Saroyan was affected by Carol's helpless tears outside his hotel room suggests that, even at the beginning, it was his sense of her deeper vulnerabilities, more than her other attractions, that decisively bound her to him. He was a famous American writer. She was a glamorous society girl whose best friends were American royalty. Yet each was like an imposter at the ball. For they were both, to a certain degree, going on their nerve—while all of those around them seemed to have deeper and more natural claims to the world in which they lived.

Several months before they were married, on September 30, 1942, in New York, Saroyan inscribed a copy of *The Trouble with Tigers* to his future wife:

> For Carol
> whose trouble
> is mine
> with love
> Bill

which may be read both as an expression of his love and, just possibly, as an early realization of a direct parallel in the problematic style of both their lives.

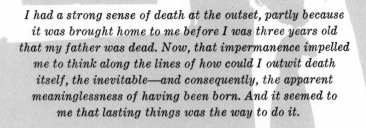

I had a strong sense of death at the outset, partly because it was brought home to me before I was three years old that my father was dead. Now, that impermanence impelled me to think along the lines of how could I outwit death itself, the inevitable—and consequently, the apparent meaninglessness of having been born. And it seemed to me that lasting things was the way to do it.

—William Saroyan
(Growing up in Fresno, *recorded interviews, 1976.*
California State University at Fresno.)

PART TWO

6

MIDLIFE CRISIS

THE onset of his middle years, his marriage to Carol Marcus, and induction in the army all seem to have combined to precipitate in Saroyan a genuine midlife crisis. More specifically, these three concurrent events seem to have broken his rhythm and, both psychologically and professionally, to have cast him adrift. The fact that he was never able to recover from this crisis either in his career or in his personal life, and that instead its effects only seemed to deepen during the more than thirty-five years of his remaining life, is a measure of its profound depth. It would also seem to point to a fundamental rigidity in Saroyan's character, an enduring manifestation perhaps of the psychic freeze discussed.

.　　　.　　　.

AFTER witnessing Carol's tears in his suite at the Hampshire House, the thirty-four-year-old Saroyan drove across the country to be inducted into the army. On the way to the West Coast, he phoned Carol from Montana and asked her if she would come out to San Francisco to meet his family. He spoke to Rosheen and consented to her suggestion that Carol should have a chaperone on her visit. Somehow, Carol and Oona O'Neill managed to convince Rosheen that they should go together—in effect, unchaperoned.

Charles Marcus, on the other hand, was opposed from the outset to his stepdaughter's involvement with Saroyan. He told Carol he didn't think the writer possessed any male protective instinct toward her and that this quality was what he looked for in a first-rate man. But his wishes were overridden.

With Carol's arrival on the West Coast, Saroyan seriously recommitted himself to their relationship. He introduced her and Oona to his mother, his grandmother, Lucy, and his unmarried sister, Cosette. Of the three, only Lucy seems to have responded favorably to the young women. She found them delightfully pretty.

Bill now told Carol he wanted to marry her. But he explained that when an Armenian man took a wife, it was very important to him that he also be able to found a family. Therefore, he asked if she would agree to get pregnant before they married so he could be certain she could bear children. Carol protested that she was young and healthy and that she was sure she could have children. Nevertheless, she eventually consented to do as Bill had asked. The affair was recommenced; and now after intercourse Bill would ask Carol to prop her legs up against a wall beside the bed, since he believed this would better the chances for conception.

THEN the writer had to report to Sacramento for basic training. For the two weeks when he wasn't allowed to have visitors, he put up Oona and Carol in a room at the Senator Hotel in Sacramento, so that Carol would be close at hand for a visit at the earliest possible date. He also asked Carol to write him a letter each day.

The eighteen-year-old girl, now settled in the hotel room with her girlfriend, and on the verge of marriage to a famous American writer almost twice her age, suddenly panicked. What was she supposed to write to William Saroyan? She wanted it to be brilliant and original, but somehow she couldn't think of anything—nothing, at any rate, that seemed to measure up to the stature of her correspondent.

Oona, meanwhile, had been receiving long, densely written, and often witty letters from a beau in New York, a young and still unknown writer named Jerry Salinger. As the two friends discussed Carol's problem of writing to Bill, it occurred to Oona that they might find exactly the sort of thing they needed in Salinger's letters.

The idea took fire. Suddenly, the floor of their hotel room was littered with the pages of Jerry Salinger's letters, while Oona, down on her knees and pen in hand, called out and marked each appropriately witty line. At the same time, Carol sat at a table composing her letters to Bill—a single page for each day—and peppering them with Salinger's witticisms. "I've just sent my typewriter to the laundry," the young writer had written to Oona. Now Oona called this out to Carol at her desk. "I've just sent my typewriter to the laundry," wrote Carol, in turn, to Bill. She felt both deeply relieved and delighted to appear so witty.

CAROL was in for a rude surprise the day of her first visit to Saroyan during his basic training. She found the man she was supposed to marry strangely subdued and formal when they met in the crowded recreation room at the base. At Saroyan's bidding, she followed him out of the room and across the street into an empty office. There, in privacy, after some stilted and, to Carol, entirely baffling exchanges, it became clear that Saroyan had been completely unnerved by the letters she had sent him. He had taken her for an innocent young girl, he told her, and now he had discovered that she was only just another clever, literary type of woman like those he had known throughout his career—the last sort of woman in the world with whom he would ever wish to be seriously involved.

Carol, in shock, began to blurt out that the letters had been largely copied from letters written by a beau of Oona's, but Saroyan brought her up short. Don't lie about it, he told her, because if there was anything in the world he hated even more than the clever and literary, it was a liar.

Carol, her emotions in knots, went away from this visit feeling numb. She and Oona packed their bags and took a train to Los Angeles. There they stayed with a friend named Martha Stevenson, once the widow of the bandleader Hal Kemp and now in the process of divorcing Victor Mature.

It was on this visit that Oona (whose father, Eugene O'Neill, lived in Contra Costa County but had refused to see her when she wrote him that she was in California) met Charles Chaplin, the man she would marry. Carol stayed in Los Angeles only briefly and returned by herself to New York.

SEVERAL months later, Saroyan called Carol in New York and asked her to see him again. And when she complied, he unexpectedly renewed his commitment to marry her. On a snowy night in February 1943 in Dayton, Ohio, where Saroyan was stationed with the Signal Corps, the couple was married by a justice of the peace, with Carol's mother, Rosheen, in attendance. Carol was now, as Bill had wanted, pregnant.

They now took up residence in a penthouse apartment at 2 Sutton Place in Manhattan, and from here Bill commuted to his current army base at Astoria, Long Island. During this period, the writer found himself so frustrated by his military regimen—despite the unusual arrangement—that he attempted to convince his superiors to discharge him on the grounds that he was mentally unfit. Just how he went about this is not known, but he was resourceful enough to prompt the army to admit him to a Section 8 ward for observation. In fact, he was under observation at the same time that his first child, this writer, was born on September 25, 1943.

Eventually, however, Bill was released from the ward, and it was the army's judgment that, although he was "paranoid" and "manic depressive," his mental condition did not warrant his being excused from military service; and their report apparently included the suggestion that the writer was, at least to some degree, pretending to be crazy. Bill replied that someone who pretends to be crazy is even crazier than a person who actually *is* crazy. Nevertheless, soon after the birth of his son, whom he and Carol named Aram, Bill's favorite Armenian name, he was shipped overseas.

IN London, where he was stationed with the film division of the Signal Corps, Bill frequently played poker with a group that, at one time or another, included the writer Irwin Shaw, the film director George Stevens (whom Bill recognized as a master of the game), and the war photographer Robert Capa. The game was sometimes interrupted by an attack of German buzz-bombs, and years later Saroyan would recall that, finding himself unable to keep the game going while most of his companions

Carol, Rosheen Marcus, Aram Saroyan. New York. 1944. (Photograph by G. Maillard Kesslere.)

Bill and his cousin Ross Bagdasarian (second from right)*, with whom he later cooperated on "Come On-a My House"* (see Chapter 10). *Paris. 1945.*

rushed for cover in the basement, he would go up to the roof with Capa to observe the city under siege. He seems to have found the war, in all ways, no more than an interruption he was obliged to tolerate.

Saroyan was by nature extremely anti-authoritarian—at least when the authority was aimed at him. Perhaps it was partly for this reason that during his tour of duty with the army, he never attained a rank above private first class and was eventually demoted back to buck private. Considering his fame at the time, this seems to have been something of an achievement in itself. He remarked later that there were others he knew who had used their celebrity to get "soft" jobs or higher rank, but that he personally found this offensive. It is possible that he would resist such special treatment because it would almost necessarily involve his feeling beholden to someone, a position he seems to have found psychologically uncomfortable.

E V E N so, Saroyan maintained that he eventually managed to make a deal with the army. He was to write a novel portraying the Allied effort, and on its completion, as his reward, he would be given an extended leave to go home to New York to visit Carol and Aram.

Saroyan worked hard on the novel, *The Adventures of Wesley Jackson* (1946), and writing it may have helped to see him through this period just before the Allied invasion of Europe. He lived at the Savoy Hotel in London while he worked, but even so, during this period of accelerated effort —he completed the novel in thirty-eight days—his physical health was unsteady.

Saroyan was now thirty-five, about the age his father was when he died. It seems likely an awareness of that fact contributed directly and significantly to his midlife malaise. As if to avoid his father's failure, he had avoided paying serious attention to the substance of Armenak's life. But now, paradoxically, Saroyan seemed fated to live out a contemporary version of that failure, with the major difference that the writer managed to stay alive. Like Armenak before him, Saroyan found himself suddenly in a new season of his life, called upon to change—and it appears to have all but killed him.

In effect, with the coming of the war years, the particular kind of soft-focus yet exuberant romanticism that had once made him so popular went decisively out of style. As a consequence of both this and the apparent rigidity of his own nature, Saroyan now went into an eclipse, professionally and personally, from which he was never to fully emerge.

In the end, perhaps it was writing that made the critical difference and kept him alive. Certainly, he approached his work at this time with intense appetite. In addition to writing the novel, he kept a journal during the days of its composition, which was later published in a single volume with *The Adventures of Wesley Jackson*, entitled *The Adventures of William Saroyan*. (The double book volume was called *The Twin Adventures*.) At the same time, he kept a voluminous private diary and wrote long daily letters to Carol.

The regimented life he knew as a soldier, inside the largely impersonal institution of the army, may have seemed to Saroyan an adult reprise of his orphanage experience, and his suffering, under the circumstances, should not be underestimated. The fact that he accomplished the amount of writing he did while under such psychological strain, tenaciously keeping to his schedule for the novel in spite of shaky health, suggests the support and refuge he found in writing during times of trouble.

With regard to the novel itself, Edmund Wilson wrote that, although he found the first part to contain a "new element of relative realism,"[1] the last part of *The Adventures of Wesley Jackson* ". . . is the record of an appalling victory over Saroyan's realistic instincts of the impulse toward self-befuddling and self-protective fantasy."[2] Writing of the young American soldier who is the hero of the novel, he continues:

> Wesley Jackson, who talks constantly of his trust in God, is specially exempted from misfortune by a darling old Providence who adores him. When he picks up what appears to be a tart in Piccadilly Circus, she turns out to be a sweet little golden-haired seventeen-year-old girl who has run away from home and who, never having slept with a man, is trying pathetically to qualify as a prostitute. Wesley takes her home to his rooms (God quickly got him out of barracks), gives her a bath and makes her his wife, and they are soon to have a baby, to which Wesley looks forward with tears in his eyes. At last he is sent to France. But don't be alarmed for a minute. Two of his best friends are killed, to be sure, but this becomes a very beautiful thing; and when he is captured by the Germans, they prove charming and presently run away, leaving their prisoners in the camp, from which Wesley

escapes back to England. He is pretty well scared for a moment when he discovers that his house has been bombed, but of course his little blue-eyed bride had luckily gone away to the country the night just before this happened, and he finds her safe and sound with her people. Even when Wesley buys tips on the races, both the horses he bets on wins, and the good old tipster is so delighted!³

Even so, in marking the shift from the felicity and ease of the first half of his career to the more ponderous character of his later work, *The Adventures of Wesley Jackson* is perhaps the pivotal book. In both *My Name Is Aram* and *The Human Comedy,* he had effectively approximated the form of the novel by interweaving a series of short stories. Indeed, one senses that running the long miles of this novel is an exhausted and disheartened sprinter. Saroyan's characteristic lightness of touch, the quick play of his mind, always a primary dimension of his charm as a writer, is gone. And in its place there is a kind of dogged piety—not so much a specific emotion as a mask that enables him to dispense with specific emotions.

By the time he had completed the book, Saroyan apparently desperately needed the leave he said he had been promised. If it was true that *The Adventures of Wesley Jackson* was something other than a celebration of the Allied effort (Irwin Shaw wrote in his review of the novel on the front page of the *New York Times Book Review*: "He [Saroyan] forgives the Germans Dachau and Belsen without blinking an eye, but he cannot forgive the sergeant who assigned him to K.P. in New York City"),⁴ nevertheless, it was his longest work to date and he had invested in it all the discipline and physical stamina he possessed.

However, according to Saroyan, the army now welshed on its promise, and the writer was denied his leave. As a direct consequence, Saroyan, as he later described it, "went berserk."⁵*

---

* During their marriage, Bill admitted to Carol that he consciously altered facts in his own journal to suit his fancy, and in this instance, similarly, the writer may have constructed in retrospect a rationale for the earlier incident in which he was admitted to a Section 8 ward. Carol cannot recall that he had any specific understanding with the army regarding a leave after he completed his book.

7

MARRIAGE, SAROYAN–STYLE

A F T E R being honorably discharged from the army at Fort Lewis, Washington, in September 1945, Saroyan, at thirty-seven, encountered for the first time day-to-day domesticity of marriage with Carol. The couple and their two-year-old son, Aram, settled into a house on Taraval Street in San Francisco, while another house, which they had designed with an architect, was being built for them in the same city. Then, in January 1946, Carol gave birth to their second and last child, a daughter they named Lucy after Saroyan's grandmother.

At Taraval Street, the couple lived only a mile or two from Bill's mother, Takoohi, and his sister Cosette, who lived together in the house the writer had bought at the top of the Sunset District. Before they settled at the Taraval Street house, however, Bill had wanted to be even closer to them. He told Carol he wanted to buy a property they had looked at in Los

Gatos with two houses on it. As he envisioned it, one of these houses would be for the two women relatives and for the children Carol produced, whom the two women would be responsible for raising. The other house would be for himself and Carol. His young wife was horrified at this idea and told him that she wanted to raise their children herself. The couple had the first big fight of their married life. Eventually the idea was abandoned.

Whatever difficulties Carol may have had as a young wife and mother, some of them directly attributable to her youth and inexperience, she seems to have had more or less conventional instincts regarding marriage and family life. Whereas Saroyan, who, particularly in later years liked to portray himself as a simple man who had had the misfortune of getting tangled up with a society girl, was in fact—as his suggestion about raising their children indicates—by far the less conventional marriage partner.

Perhaps because in his own experience Saroyan had encountered no example of the role a family man plays on a day-to-day basis (Takoohi had never remarried and does not seem to have even entertained suitors), he approached the idea of family life with an erratic and complex set of impulses that he was never able to adapt into a workable domestic routine. Indeed, marriage and a family appear to have been little more than abstractions for Saroyan. Having known less of their reality in his own history than even his wife, Carol, had known in hers, he nevertheless boldly applied to them—as if boldness might mask his uncertainty—a set of principles and ideals that he seems to have borrowed piecemeal from other areas of his life and from the Armenian and American scene at large.

The first of these was the importance, stressed in the old country, of founding a family, which the writer had emphasized to Carol. But that he would all but insist that she get pregnant before he would marry her smacks of a curious, *new*-world sort of biological materialism. This impersonal emphasis is further underscored by his desire to live alone in one house with Carol, while his female relatives lived next door, charged with the care of the children his wife would breed. In fact, this domestic structure seems an architectural restatement of Saroyan's Fresno childhood experience of "good" and "bad" women: the first confined to the kitchen and the second to the bedroom.

As in Saroyan's literary work, there is a peculiar application here of principles normally associated with American industrial efficiency: an emphasis on product and quantity—for Saroyan envisioned an enormous

Carol and Aram. San Francisco. c. 1947.

Aram and Lucy. Taraval Street. c. 1948.

Bill with kitten. Taraval Street. c. 1947.

family once he had his set-up in place—apparently unchecked by any sense that the more traditional values of marriage and family might be undermined by such an impersonal separation of functions.

T H E temporary house at Taraval Street was set up so that Saroyan could have his office on the top floor, above and out of the way of the normal chaos of a household with two small children. Even so, not long after the family had settled into the house, Saroyan came downstairs from his office and told Carol he was having trouble writing. The writer explained to his young wife that for him to do the kind of work he had always done, and for which he had become celebrated, he needed to have the same kind of working conditions he had had when he produced this work. What was missing now, he explained, was the pressure of "a handicap," something to energize him fully so that he could then overcome it. He had always worked *against* the odds, whereas his current situation as a writer who was respected by the critics, successful financially, and now settling down into the domestic routine of a family man simply lacked the kind of risk that had brought forth his best work. Therefore, the writer told his wife, he needed to gamble.

Carol reasoned to herself that if Bill wasn't able to write, no matter what the rest of their marriage might be like, he wouldn't love her. For this reason, she agreed to let Bill go ahead and gamble.

Using a bookie, the writer now commenced to bet on six horse races a day at $5,000 a race. At the same time, almost every night the couple—for Bill liked having Carol with him—left the children in the care of their housekeeper and went to an illegal gambling establishment in San Francisco known as Russian Mike's where Carol would sit at a table with Bill, who periodically got up and played high-stakes roulette, baccarat, and blackjack.

BROADLY speaking, Saroyan's gambling venture could have had three possible results, all of which contain a psychological common denominator. One possibility, as unlikely as it might be, was that Saroyan would defy all the odds and be a consistent winner at the track and the casino: that he would demonstrate the kind of luck that might be said to constitute earthly evidence of divine grace. A second possibility was that Saroyan would lose, but that then, according to plan, he would be inspired to excel in his creative work. Saroyan's gambling losses would prove to have been only the first, necessary step—one with no lasting negative effect—in a process of creative alchemy. As a direct result of his gambling losses, the writer would find himself working at the top of his form. Once again, he would prove—this time in the form of creative inspiration—that he was on the receiving end of a kind of divine grace.

This is the equation Saroyan had worked out for himself, and it might be said to have had a certain validity during the early years of his career. With talent, persistence, and luck, he had surmounted the odds of his orphaned childhood, as well as the poverty and deprivation of his youth, to become a famous writer. However, there were social, political, and economic factors working fortuitously in his favor at the time. Besides these, he possessed the psychological and physical resources of robust youth. Now, though, there was a new mood in both the nation and the world, and, at the same time, Saroyan's youth had ended. Perhaps this is the reason why it was the third possibility that became the reality: Saroyan lost heavily and continued to lose heavily, without making up for his losses through his creative work.

SINCE Saroyan eventually exceeded his own considerable financial resources—in fact, this seems from the beginning to have been a part of his scheme to revive his creativity—implicit in this third possibility was the appearance of someone who would pay off his debts.

Hence this third possibility, like the other two, provided evidence that Saroyan was different from other people, if not by virtue of his luck as a gambler or his creative inspiration as a writer, then by virtue of the fact that he was important enough to have someone take over the burden of his debt and get him out of trouble. And, in fact, Saroyan was able to find someone to take on this role: the San Francisco restaurateur George Mardikian, the owner of Omar Khayam's, a well-known Armenian restaurant the writer liked to frequent. However, Mardikian was not a man to engage in outright charity, even for his celebrated countryman, and by the time Saroyan's gambling forays were over, the restaurateur held the deed to both Saroyan's Taraval Street house and the additional property that he had bought in San Francisco, along with the architect's plans for it.

In a certain sense, all three solutions had only one meaning: they would all testify to Saroyan's being a special case, a chosen one—if not a godlike irreversible force at the gambling table or the typewriter, then a childlike eminence who would be rescued from the mishap that had befallen him.

ALL three solutions, in turn, are evidence of a psychological condition in Saroyan that, with the end of youth, would become increasingly prominent. In characterizing this condition, it should be recalled that the writer experienced the trauma of the death of his father and the subsequent confinement in an orphanage before his third birthday, a time when he had yet to master language.

Following Freud, it may be said of a child of this age and at this level of language development that both the id (the child) and the superego (the parent) play more prominent roles in the child's psychological life than the just emerging, still rather tentative ego (the adult).

Curiously enough, such a condition seems to characterize Saroyan's gambling forays. Thus, there is apparent a strong personal identification in the writer with the superego—that is, with the parent figure in the form of luck, inspiration, or, failing those, someone who will bail him out—in all three cases a kind of beneficent God-the-father; and an identification with the id—that is, with the child given free rein to indulge his appetites. Strangely absent here, however, is any clear sense of his identification with a functioning, mediating ego: an adult who acknowledges the perils of, and assumes responsibility for, his actions.

BY the same token, Saroyan sometimes tends to speak in his work with the voice of a benevolent oracle, on occasion sounding as if he himself were the God he originally had imagined to be the author of all books. Had he imagined this, after all, only because, given the possibility of his own arrested ego function, he could not conceive of a book written by a mere adult? If this was the case, it may have been necessary for Saroyan to become the beneficent father himself in order to be a writer. However presumptuous such a stance might appear to be, when the writer was at his best, as in his celebrated preface to *The Time of Your Life*, one would have to credit him with a strong and exhilarating impersonation:

> In the time of your life, live—so that in that good time there shall be no ugliness or death for yourself or for any life your life touches.

Seek goodness everywhere, and when it is found, bring it out of its hiding-place and let it be free and unashamed. Place in matter and in flesh the least of the values, for these are the things that hold death, and must pass away. Discover in things that which shines and is beyond corruption. Encourage virtue in whatever heart it may have been driven into secrecy and sorrow by the shame and terror of the world. Ignore the obvious, for it is unworthy of the clear eye and the kindly heart. Be the inferior of no man, nor of any man be the superior. Remember that every man is a variation of yourself. No man's guilt is not yours, nor is any man's innocence a thing apart. Despise evil and ungodliness, but not men of ungodliness or evil. These, understand. Have no shame in being kindly and gentle, but if the time comes in the time of your life to kill, kill and have no regret. In the time of your life, live—so that in that wondrous time you shall not add to the misery and sorrow of the world, but shall smile to the infinite delight and mystery of it.[1]

Amen. Yet for all its undeniable magic, one still might wonder who Saroyan could have had in mind for this piece of high-flown instruction, written at the ripe old age of thirty. On the other hand, one of the most interesting details of the writer's personality was that he remained troubled throughout his life by his rhetorical injunction in the preface: "if the time comes in the time of your life to kill, kill and have no regret." At one point, when he wrote the piece out in longhand, he changed the passage to read: "if the time comes in the time of your life to kill, kill the killers and have no regret." On other occasions, he seems to have regretted it in its entirety. The writer was also troubled by his most famous and popular novel, *The Human Comedy*, which he felt romanticized and falsified the experience of the war.

The novel was written after the screenplay, which Saroyan had sold outright to Louis B. Mayer at MGM for $60,000. When the writer discovered that he wouldn't be the film's director, which he had apparently been led to believe he would be, he offered $80,000 to buy back his rights to the property. Mayer refused and went on to make the popular movie starring Mickey Rooney. Saroyan subsequently received the Academy Award for the best original screen story of 1943, but continued to feel he had been "taken" by Mayer in a crooked deal.

The Human Comedy proved to be Saroyan's most popular book—a Book-of-the-Month Club selection that went on to become a favorite of American high school reading lists up to the present day. Perhaps because it had been first written as a screenplay, there is an emphasis on narrative incident and detail, with a minimum of the stylistic posing and padding that was to prove characteristic of Saroyan's later novels. The book moves lightly and charmingly, and reaches a climax that pulls at the heart as expertly as the Hollywood film, if not more so. Unfortunately, as Edmund Wilson piercingly observed of both the book and the film: "even when a good fellow got killed, he wasn't really and truly dead, because his spirit was still able to return (in the movie you could see him right there) and stay on with the people he loved."[2]

That Saroyan himself would eventually come to second these scruples points to a place in the writer that remained open and vulnerable to the lessons of his life, almost in spite of himself. This quality makes it clear that, whatever the evidence to the contrary, he could never be entirely dismissed as what might be called a psychologically closed-circuit (or clinically "narcissistic" personality), one whom nothing from the outside world ever genuinely reached and impressed. Sporadically, but insistently, the adult—rather than some strictly "divine" or childlike—intelligence in Saroyan would reveal itself.

TOWARD the middle of this gambling spree, Saroyan sold *The Time of Your Life* as a movie property to the Cagney brothers, who went on to make it into the film starring James Cagney. With this windfall, the writer made an apparently spur-of-the-moment move with Carol and the children to the East Coast, where he rented a house in Oyster Bay, Long Island. As it turned out, the family lived there for about six months before returning to Taraval Street.

It was during this period in the East that a curious incident occurred that further underscores Saroyan's erratic behavior within his marriage. Carol's friend Oona had come to New York with her husband, Charles Chaplin, and the two couples were eager to see each other. Bill and Carol arranged to leave the children with a housekeeper and took a train into Manhattan, where they booked a room at the Hotel Pierre for the night so they could have a late evening with the Chaplins.

That night the two couples went pub crawling, a favorite pastime of

Seated l. to r., beginning fourth and fifth from left: Charles and Oona Chaplin, Carol and Bill, Frank and Araxie Moradian. New York. 1947.

Martha Stevenson, Sam Marx, Bill, and Carol. c. 1947.

both Chaplin's and Saroyan's, and by the time Bill and Carol got back to the Pierre, it was already dawn. They had both had a wonderful time. However, when they got into bed, Bill made a lovemaking overture to Carol, who drowsily said something about its being a better idea after they had slept. At this point, Bill suddenly bolted out of bed and began to rage at Carol. All evening, he told her, she had been so charming and so beautiful, the delight of them all. But now, when she was alone with him, she was suddenly sleepy. The writer was so enraged that he put his clothes back on and left their hotel room. Carol didn't know what had happened. She had been genuinely sleepy—that was all. Why had Bill gotten so angry? And where had he gone? And when would he be coming back?

When the writer still hadn't returned by checkout time at the Pierre, Carol checked out by herself and took their scheduled train back to Oyster Bay and the children. Bill hadn't returned ahead of her. Nor did he return the next day. By now Carol had gone into a kind of bewildered mourning. Had Bill left her for good?

After four days passed, Bill called. He was in New Orleans, he told his wife, and had been thinking about her. He thought she had probably better come down there to be with him as soon as possible. Immensely relieved, Carol made arrangements to leave immediately. Their marriage hadn't ended after all.

8

THE BREAKUP

AFTER the Saroyans had returned to Taraval Street, Bill's gambling losses escalated to the point of ruin. Then one day he came down from his office and told Carol that nobody could work with the kind of debt he now had hanging over him. He had gone too far. Why had Carol allowed him to do it, Bill wanted to know. He told her that a real woman wouldn't have let her husband indulge in such madness. In effect, he blamed her for what had happened.

Perhaps in a last-ditch effort to break off his entrenched routine at Russian Mike's, Bill decided to move to the East Coast once again. This time the Saroyans rented an apartment in Manhattan, on East 58th Street near the Plaza Hotel. It was here that the couple's first marriage ended, under circumstances probably unique in marital history.

.   .   .

OVER the years of their marriage, it had weighed on Carol that Bill didn't know she was Jewish. Carol would later describe her relationship with Bill in terms of his pendulum-like mood swings: he seemed to perceive her as either an angel or a monster, and in either case his judgment seemed to have nothing whatsoever to do with the reality of the moment. Hence, it was during an evening when she sensed that she could virtually do no wrong (that the pendulum was on the positive side of its swing) that she worked up the nerve to ask Bill whether there was, in fact, anything at all that could ever make him not love her.

"No, kid," he told her, using his favorite form of address for his wife. He assured her that his love was absolutely steadfast, that nothing could ever change that. But then Bill remembered that there was, after all, *one* thing. He told Carol that the only thing in the world that could ever change his feeling for her would be if he were to find out that she was Jewish. Carol, who had asked her first question as a preliminary to a revelation of the truth, now hastily abandoned the idea.

NEVERTHELESS, her lie kept bothering her, insistently popping up at the edge of her consciousness, urging her to set her relationship with Bill right once and for all. And one night—just after the couple had made love and were lying together in bed (another occasion when Carol felt secure in Bill's positive feeling for her)—she finally took the long-postponed step and admitted to her husband that she was, in fact, Jewish.

Bill reacted immediately. He got up out of bed and arranged a pillow and blankets for himself on the living room sofa. Several hours later, however, in the middle of the night, he came back into their room, turned on the lights, and tore the covers off the bed where Carol lay naked. "Look at you," he told his wife, "all white and pink and perfect. Do you mean to tell me that you're Jewish? How can that be possible? Come on, kid. You're not Jewish. How could someone as beautiful as you are be Jewish?"

Carol now realized that she was profoundly angry. She got up from the bed and pulling a blanket around herself, she shouted at Bill, "My God, what do you think a Jew *is*? What do you think I'm supposed to look like!"

That same morning, Bill left Carol and their children and didn't return. With Carol's consent, he put through a divorce in Reno, and then sailed for Europe. It was March 1949. The Saroyans had been married a little more than six years.

T H E first question here concerns the writer's anti-Semitism, which would seem to have gone generally unrecognized, despite its shocking virulence. Saroyan's anti-Semitism is corroborated, too, by his attitude toward Hitler, whom he characterized to Carol as "a great zealot." Yet one hesitates to take any of this too strictly at face value. For one thing, other than to Carol, Saroyan generally seems to have kept his high opinion of Hitler to himself. Then too, the writer had casual but affectionate relationships with many Jews. He seems, in fact, to have been almost exclusively an anti-Semite in social situations among Armenians of his own generation, among whom anti-Semitism would seem to have been rather common and where it may have served no deeper motive than to emphasize a general camaraderie, something perhaps not uncharacteristic of such prejudice.

In the end, though, perhaps the truly decisive dimension of this episode, as well as the episode after the evening with the Chaplins, was something else entirely: specifically, that Carol had on both occasions, though in different ways, obviously displayed her own independence of mind and spirit to Bill.

In the case of the evening with the Chaplins, she had apparently behaved in a way everyone had found charming. Then, after they had gotten into bed, she had told Bill she would rather make love after they had had some sleep. Perhaps the writer simply found these two expressions of her own identity, coming one on top of the other, too much to take. Then too, his ego may already have been threatened by the evening with the Chaplins, as much as he seemed to enjoy it. For Chaplin was a giant as an artist, and Saroyan as a general rule seemed to prefer the company of those with significantly less worldly stature than he. Indeed, it was Carol's friendship with Oona that had been primary in bringing the couples together. And Carol had then been a delight that evening. Saroyan may have been wounded enough by his wife's charm in such a high-powered social situation that to then have her sleepily decline to make love was all he needed to throw him into a rage and make him walk out. Likewise, Bill's response to Carol's admission that she was Jewish—suddenly, with no apparent hesitation, ending their marriage—may have been a deeper and more complicated expression of the same rage.

.   .   .

IN THE end, Saroyan's marriage may have been fundamentally dependent on the condition that Carol's insecurities, as she had first revealed them to him by her tears at the Hampshire House, would remain deep enough for him to dominate her, that she would never threaten him as a genuine equal. If this were the case, the writer's bizarre behavior throughout the couple's relationship might make sense as a strategy of periodic psychological intimidation. If, on the one hand, Carol were to respond with anger or outrage to any one of his tactics, then Bill would know that she had now achieved independence and would no longer be an appropriately servile partner. On the other hand, as long as Carol remained vulnerable to such tactics, full of doubts about her own worth, the writer perhaps had her where he wanted her.

When he regretfully but abruptly broke off their affair at the Hampshire House, he was rewarded by an unprecedented show of tears that seems to have genuinely melted him and convinced him to reconsider. However, the cruelty of that occasion—in which Saroyan revealed a self-centered disregard for the magnitude of the young girl's commitment to him in surrendering her virginity (the near equivalent, in a forties' debutante, of the marriage vow)—would appear to have set the pattern for a series of periodic rude jolts administered by the writer as if to reaffirm Carol's psychological dependence.

The major events recounted here—the Hampshire House breakdown, the imperative pregnancy, the Salinger letters, the Chaplin evening, and the Jewish issue—were part of a pattern that was, on a less spectacular level, equally evident in the couple's day-to-day life. Carol's awareness of Bill's pendulumlike mood swings, which seemed to her to occur independently of any influence she might exert, is in essence the testimony of a person who had surrendered her equality within the relationship. However, her admission that she was Jewish, in the face of his intimidation, testified to her growing courage.

9
THE OLD-COUNTRY MUSTACHE

A T the beginning of what might be called his middle period, the forty-year-old Saroyan would find physical mobility, in both his writing and his life, important to him once again—as it had been in his early days as a newsboy and a messenger. Having broken off his marriage, he soon sailed for Europe; and once there, he returned to his habit of compulsive gambling.

In the two-year interval between his divorce and his remarriage to Carol, Saroyan's major works were his novella, *The Assyrian* (1950), a fictionalized account of his stay in Lisbon, his gambling there, and his encounter there with the Armenian multimillionaire, Gulbenkian; and the novel, *Rock Wagram* (1951), which portrays the visit of the title figure, an Armenian-American movie star whose marriage is in trouble, to his hometown, Fresno, California.

The most unsatisfying dimension of both these works is the insistent opacity of the major figure in each. Saroyan limits his characterizations almost exclusively to the physical actions of his two subjects—both clearly extensions of himself—as if by doing so he might discover some compelling inner dynamic. Yet both figures, psychologically stymied in some way the author seems to prefer not to explore, or even to acknowledge, merely skim the surface of their environment, staying in *motion* as if this were somehow the real heroism in human affairs. Likewise, the dialogue in *Rock Wagram* tends to be evasively arch or stoical, occasionally echoing the manner of Hemingway but without his conviction.

Both works might be said to fail to come to terms with, or even to recognize in any genuine way, what they are, in fact, about. In *Rock Wagram*, the writer has interspersed his narrative with italicized sections of a generalized, meditative melancholy, and these comprise the book's most memorable writing. Chapter 1, entitled "The Father," begins with one of these passages:

> Every man is a good man in a bad world. No man changes the world. Every man himself changes from good to bad or from bad to good, back and forth, all his life, and then dies. But no matter how or why or when a man changes, he remains a good man in a bad world, as he himself knows. All his life a man fights death, and then at last loses the fight, always having known he would. Loneliness is every man's portion, and failure. The man who seeks to escape from loneliness is a lunatic. The man who does not know that *all* is failure is a fool. The man who does not laugh at these things is a bore. But the lunatic is a good man, and so is the fool, and so is the bore, as each of them knows. Every man is innocent, and in the end a lonely lunatic, a lonely fool, or a lonely bore.
>
> But there is meaning to a man. There is meaning to the life every man lives. It is a secret meaning, and pathetic if it weren't for the lies of art.[1]

Unfortunately, these passages never merge, other than by vague implication, with the title figure, and the book tends to take the form of two parallel lines that never intersect.

It may be that the missing point of intersection here is the part of the psyche that seems to have failed to reach functional maturity in Saroyan's development: the adult ego that mediates between the demands of the child and the wisdom of the father. The empty center in *Rock Wagram* might be regarded as the equivalent of impaired ego development. Hence, on the one hand, there is the *movement* of the child (in the narrative's preoccupation with physical mobility), and on the other, the *reflection* of the father (in the italicized philosophical passages)—but, in between, where one might expect to encounter the socialized adult, there is a disconcerting absence.

THEN, too, so much of the charm of Saroyan's early stories lay in their characteristic exuberance. What they may have lacked in adult resonance, they more than made up for in youthful verve. Saroyan, in his first phase, was an unabashed performer. He played to his audience with genuine spirit and his own kind of street savvy. He cut a figure—and that figure had become a star.

In the very act of performing as an artist, of being the celebrated, daring young man of his prewar career, Saroyan may have come as close as he would ever come to achieving psychological equilibrium. Having such a strong intuitive sense of how to approach and disarm his audience, and having thereby succeeded in capturing their devotion, Saroyan could now work in a climate of emotional support. His ego, however weakly developed, would now be bolstered by the adulation of his public. But when the mood changed, and the writer's particular style of performing lost favor, Saroyan would suffer more than the commonplace necessity among entertainers periodically to renew and restructure an act. For in losing favor as a performer, he was also losing what was perhaps an essential psychological support system.

THIS middle period was essentially the period of the writer as a novelist. Perhaps because he sensed a need for a weightier form to satisfy his public's changed attitude, Saroyan, during the next fifteen years, published a succession of novels that were for the most part dark and broodingly serious, not to say portentous: *Rock Wagram* (1951), *The Laughing Matter* (1953), *Boys and Girls Together* (1963), and *One Day in the Afternoon of the World* (1964).

Only in the novella *Tracy's Tiger* (1951) and the novel *Mama, I Love*

You (1956), dedicated to his daughter Lucy and narrated by a seven-year-old girl, does one catch a glimpse of the writer's former spark. The problem was not deficiency of craft. Saroyan was almost always a careful prose writer, and many of these books contain admirable passages. Yet over all there is a slackness—and a paradoxical tightness at the heart of it. Many of the books read as if Saroyan decided to write a novel and then, page by page, carried out his decision with little motive beyond the salutary exercise of discipline.

Perhaps the most fundamental problem was that, given Saroyan's psychological makeup, the novel would almost inevitably seem to be the least congenial of literary forms for him. The socially engaged ego seems to have been virtually dormant in him. In the era of Depression and world war, of fascism and communism, he remained singularly aloof, later describing himself as "a spiritual anarchist." In his best work, he wrote with a kind of childlike—or, alternately, godlike—clarity, exuberance, and beneficence. But in his novels, where he attempts to chronicle the life of an adult man in the actual world of his day, there is a stilted, unrealized feeling. One senses that the writer is striking poses rather than writing out of his own real nature. Indeed, the reader may grow restless for a sign of the showman and his familiar pyrotechnics. For in him, at least, one knew the delight of the engaged performer, the entertainer who relished each moment before the crowd.

The showman, however, had now had a taste of failure, both publicly and personally, and he harbored a certain bitterness against both his public and his critics. Here the difficulty the writer may have known because of weak ego-development is further underscored. A person whose ego is functioning poorly would seem to have only the most cursory, sketchy sense of the world outside himself. The scarcity of palpable physical detail in almost all of Saroyan's later writing is one possible signature of this condition. Another might be found in the writer's general inability to create fully realized characters. When Saroyan's characters speak, especially in these novels, one is frequently reminded of an interview, as opposed to actual dialogue. Perhaps the most extreme instance of this is the novel *Papa, You're Crazy*, which Saroyan dedicated to this writer, and which is made up almost entirely of discussions between a father and his young son. Unfortunately, in none of these conversations does either figure emerge in anything like full human dimension. For the most part, the son asks stilted, childlike questions and the father makes stilted, godlike pronouncements in reply: a structure perhaps doomed from the outset to underscore Saroyan's psychological and literary weak-link:

> "Pop, is everybody dissatisfied?"
>
> "No doubt about it. All his life a man is at least a little dissatisfied with everything, beginning with his parents, his world, his time, his country, his government, and then moving along to himself and his past and his present and perhaps his children and his friends and their children, because it *is* in this animal's nature to aspire, and therefore to fail, and then to find fault and to be dissatisfied. But we've got to remember that even while he *is* finding fault and being dissatisfied, he is also feeling pretty good and being at least half-proud of himself."[2]

Then, too, if the ego is fundamentally weak, if its condition is more or less constitutionally imperiled, it would seem to need constant reassurance of one sort or another. Writing itself seems to have assumed something of this function for Saroyan. In addition, he apparently took some comfort in his own self-willed demonstrations of literary discipline, speed, and tenacity. And, no doubt, he was psychologically bolstered by the fame and success he had achieved, even if sometimes he felt creatively hampered by it.

Aside from public adulation, however, Saroyan could not count on the actual world of day-to-day reality to help support his threatened ego. In fact, it is in this arena that all egos take their daily knocks, and their resilience is perhaps a primary sign of fundamental health. But in Saroyan's case a different pattern emerges. After a social outing with his wife, where he would often be the hit of the occasion, holding forth with seemingly endless energy and charm, Saroyan would take to his bed for literally days in order to recover. His physical and emotional resources had been exhausted by his performance. Nevertheless, Saroyan seemed to find it a psychological necessity to command the center of attention on all such occasions to which he committed himself.

THE writer was not, in truth, a man who often formed friendships. He knew people who were more or less incidental to his own social activities—restaurateurs, headwaiters, bookies, bartenders—people with whom his relationship was determined largely by their services to him. Although Saroyan would on occasion cultivate such people as if they were equals, if one of them were actually to assume such an equality, as a general rule the writer doesn't seem to have been gratified.

During the first year of his marriage, when his Signal Corps regiment was stationed at Astoria, Long Island, and he commuted to the army each morning from the apartment he and Carol had taken on Sutton Place in Manhattan, Saroyan arrived home one evening with a fellow private, who was a photographer. He had asked this man, a slightly built Armenian, to take some photographs of Carol and him. After taking a few preliminary shots, however, the man got caught up in talking with his host and his host's wife, and put the camera aside for the moment. When he did pick it up again, he took only a few more photographs before resuming conversation. Carol, in the meantime, had become aware that Bill was growing furious, and, in an effort to avoid a blow-up, grew more and more mute, trying to indicate to the photographer that he should cut short his talking and take more photographs. The photographer, perhaps gauchely but no doubt innocently, had assumed that Saroyan was genuinely interested in who he was, rather than in simply having him take the photographs and go. In a few more moments, the writer exploded at the little man and all but threw him out of the apartment.

Nor was Saroyan interested in friendships with his professional peers, either in person or in correspondence. He did have casual friendships with fellow writers, but rarely if ever did these deepen into either a genuine intimacy or a serious dialogue of any kind. Rather, Saroyan seems to have preferred the company of his cousins and other relatives for his more intimate social life. And even these family relationships were subject to his up-and-down mood swings. Once, while they were living at Taraval Street, Carol arranged for a surprise birthday party for Bill, inviting Takoohi and Cosette, Zabelle and her husband, Walter Papazian, and their children, as well as a number of the writer's favorite cousins. But when Bill entered the house and his relatives surrounded him yelling "Surprise!" the writer went into a rage and shouted at them to get out—which, stunned into silence, they all did. "Don't you ever do that again!" Saroyan yelled after them.

Nor did Saroyan maintain contact with his literary peers, with society, or history, through serious reading. At best, he was a browser, and seldom if ever read a book from cover to cover.

. . .

T A K E N as a whole, these social and literary habits had the effect of severely limiting Saroyan's intellectual and personal growth. Having managed to insulate himself in this way from the deeper levels of life and learning, even as he aged it was difficult for him to achieve a genuine maturity. Rather, he continued to play the "character," the literary maverick or desperado—and, as the years went by, this role seemed by subtle stages to alter itself, so that he increasingly came to be regarded as a kind of benign eccentric.

I T was during the period between his marriages, too, that the writer first grew the large mustache that was to become the trademark of his later persona. Like the novels he was now writing, it may also have testified to Saroyan's recognition that his public image was in need of a weightier resonance. However, again like the novels, it was more as if the writer was striking a more profound pose than that he was authentically maturing. Suddenly the daring young man was wearing an old-country mustache, the same sort of mustache his father Armenak had worn.

In seeking an explanation for this change in his appearance, it should be remembered that the fact that he was Armenian made a unique difference in the degree of his celebrity among the people of his own nationality. The Armenians, a people of relatively small number, whose ranks had recently been subjected to both genocide and the loss of their independence as a nation, perhaps understandably regarded their famous author, who spoke for them, as a being approaching godhood. In effect, the American-born writer, with his complex and wounded personality, became for the Armenians almost an object of worship. And Saroyan would increasingly come to depend on this reverence to bolster and restore him periodically. He first visited Soviet Armenia in 1935, right after his first success, and he made three or four more visits, the last near the end of his life.

He had become very likely the most famous man in the entire history of his people, partly because of the small number of Armenians and partly because he happened to live in an era of global communications. And even after his fame and impact as an American writer began to wane, and he had lost a good deal of his following and suffered the disparagement or neglect of the critics, Armenians throughout the world remained steadfast

The old-country style mustache. Saroyan with his cousin Archie Minasian. San Francisco. 1949. (Photograph courtesy of Archie Minasian.)

in their loyalty. Saroyan was able to count on them for assurance that he was a great man no matter what the rest of the world might say. Over the long run, of course, this unqualified veneration did him little good, either personally or professionally.

However, the writer's large, old-country-style mustache, grown for the first time after his first divorce from Carol, may have represented Saroyan's growing emotional allegiance to the Armenians: it may have been an implicit, and perhaps unconscious, acknowledgment of the importance to him of their devotion. In a sense, with this change in his appearance, Saroyan turned from the new world, America, which seemed to be deserting him, back to the old world of his forefathers, Armenia, which remained constant in honoring him.

Interestingly enough, by the time he remarried Carol, an act that might be read as a turning back toward America, he had shaved the mustache off—only to grow it back on again, this time for good, after their second divorce.

10

THE SECOND TIME AROUND

DURING the period in and around Saroyan's second marriage to and divorce from Carol Marcus, the writer gave increasing evidence of what is identified in post-Freudian psychoanalysis as narcissistic personality disorder. Such people commonly achieve a high level of worldly success. All of them have a strong tendency to regard others as mere psychological props.[1] Bill's behavior with Carol during this period might serve as a case in point. He left his twenty-four-year-old wife and their two children, apparently without the slightest qualm or concern for their future welfare. On the very morning he left, his three-year-old daughter, Lucy, was in the hospital recovering from a tonsilectomy.

In Europe, the writer gambled with customary abandon—at times, his flagrant gambling would in itself seem to be a narcissistically self-aggrandizing extravagance—but he didn't send Carol any money for herself or the children, and his ex-wife was eventually desperate enough for money to take a job as an office "go-fer." She was soon fired from the job. Mortified by her failure, and now running a high fever, she decided to try to reach Bill in Paris, where she had heard he was currently living. She phoned a long list of Paris hotels, asking for him at each one. When, at last, at one hotel her call was put through and she was connected to Bill in his room, on hearing her voice he went into a rage and hung up.

Eventually, she and the children were evicted from the East 58th Street apartment, a circumstance that made headlines in the New York papers. She now moved into an apartment with an old girlfriend from her school days, Leila Hadley. It was during this period that she began to see a man with whom she was to become seriously involved. Like Saroyan, the man was a public figure considerably older than she; but unlike the writer, he was both rich and romantically devoted. The young divorcée ultimately fell in love with him, and he asked her to marry him.

Saroyan had in the meantime come back from Europe, lived in the San Francisco house he had bought for his mother (where he grew his first mustache and wrote *Rock Wagram*), and returned to Europe for a second visit. Then, after having more or less ignored both Carol and his children, he became aware that his ex-wife was involved with another man. This news seems to have catalyzed a transformation in his emotional life.

SUDDENLY, Bill was in New York and he had to see Carol again. She herself was happy to have him visit their children but preferred not to see him alone. The writer had his ex-wife followed by a private detective. He then enlisted the support of his old friend Artie Shaw, who had originally introduced him to Carol, as well as that of his cousin Ross Bagdasarian, who was also a friend of Carol's, asking them to speak to his ex-wife on his behalf, which they did.

As a result, Carol agreed to meet Bill by herself. With apparent astonishment, he now learned directly from her that she was having an affair with, and was in love with, another man. Nevertheless, he told Carol that he wanted her back. Carol replied that she was no longer in love with him. "Of course you're not," Bill told her, "you have no reason to be. But give me a chance. You will be."

Thus began, essentially for the first time (since during their first phase, Carol had been smitten from the beginning), Bill's courtship of Carol. And indeed, the writer assumed the role of suitor with no little flair. Years later, Carol would recall Bill's special ability to put romantic feeling into just the right words when he spoke to her over a candlelit dinner.

AT the very beginning of this period, an incident occurred that casts considerable light on Carol's psychological state with regard to her ex-husband. During the late afternoon of a day on which she planned to give a cocktail party for her friend, the former Martha Stevenson, who had recently married, Bill, having just returned that day from the first of two visits to Europe, arrived unexpectedly at her door. Carol invited him in. The writer soon noticed that the dining room table was covered with glasses and that there were many arrangements of flowers throughout the apartment, and he asked Carol if she were planning to give a party. Still under the thrall of Bill's unpredictable moods with regard to social occasions, Carol found herself baldly denying it.

Just as when she had denied she was Jewish, a sort of psychic cat-and-mouse game now ensued. Bill seems to have sensed that he had again forced Carol into a self-destructive deception, and he lingered in the apartment as the evening wore on, periodically returning to the question of the party, which he correctly assumed was imminent. But Carol, finding herself ensnared in this psychological ambush brought on by her own defensiveness with Bill, nevertheless stuck to her guns and insisted that there was to be no party. With the arrival time of the guests perilously close, Bill now fortuitously excused himself to use the bathroom and Carol, in a panic, called the doorman downstairs and asked him to tell any visitors who might arrive that she had gone out and not to allow them to come up to the apartment. She then called Martha to tell her to call the guests and tell them the party was off. At Carol's bidding, Bill eventually helped himself to drinks. Finally, late in the evening, he departed, now perhaps genuinely bewildered.

Carol, then, remained frightened of Bill, yet, at the same time, she seems to have found in him a kind of psychological prototype that may have answered an internal need of her own. For she was a young woman who had never known her own actual father; and at the age of eight her existence had been completely transformed, as in a fairy tale, by a stepfather who, at forty-nine, might have more likely been a grandfather to her. Then,

Carol and Bill. San Francisco. c. 1947.

Carol and Bill. New York. 1950.

while still essentially an adolescent, she had married a world-famous man who, although considerably younger than Charles Marcus, was nonetheless fully twice her age. The gap in their ages was closer to the one customary between a parent and a child. Indeed, Bill was the same age as Carol's mother, Rosheen.

If, in the ensuing years, Saroyan had proved to be an impossible husband, nevertheless his presence may have served, however problematically, to animate what Carol, in her heart still a fatherless orphan, might have otherwise experienced only as a desolating absence. In this way, he would be salutary for her, almost in spite of himself. Moreover, that Carol eventually agreed to remarry Bill after the wrenching failure of their first marriage—even when another and kinder man wanted to marry her— perhaps indicates that she was still in the throes of a prolonged psychological and spiritual adolescence.[2] At one moment, she was ready to assume her own full-fledged adult independence and in the next she was still hesitant, preferring to test herself for a while longer in the arena that Bill, with his insistent and almost maniacal paternalism, provided by a kind of unwitting proxy.

Then, too, there were the couple's two young children and the momentary, extravagant hope, very likely on both their parts, that somehow the family could be healed and restored.

T H E couple was remarried in Beverly Hills in March 1951, two years to the month after their separation, and they lived, together with Aram and Lucy and a housekeeper-governess Carol had brought with her from New York, at 708 North Rodeo Drive, where Bill had rented a two-storey, Spanish-style stucco home with an orange tiled roof.

I M M E D I A T E L Y after their wedding, Bill and Carol went on a honeymoon cruise to Catalina with the Chaplins on their yacht. It was while on the boat that Bill happened to pick up a new book, which he read with mounting delight. "This kid's really got it," he reported to Carol and Oona and Charlie. With a smile, Oona replied that Bill hadn't thought so in Sacramento. The book was J. D. Salinger's novel, *The Catcher in the Rye*.

F R O M the outset, the second marriage went badly. Whatever her uncertainties may have been, Carol had, during the course of the two years they had been apart, acquired a stronger sense of her own autonomy, almost automatically putting her at odds with Bill's tendency to play the—often irrational—autocrat.

It is one of the genuinely touching paradoxes of Saroyan's life that, given his rigidly authoritarian inclinations, he would marry the fundamentally spirited and strong-willed young woman he did. He might have easily found a young Armenian woman who would have felt it not just a duty, but an honor, to wait on him hand and foot for the rest of his days. Instead, Saroyan, unlike many of his Armenian contemporaries, made the jump into the American melting pot with a young woman who was the opposite of all that he would seem to have desired in a wife.

And when the marriage turned out to be a disaster, and he had learned with no uncertainty just how great a chasm existed between himself and Carol, he nevertheless came back a second time, and seemingly by sheer force of will made the marriage happen again. But equally, as was indicated before, this self-willed second marriage has a dimension to it that suggests an ego-gratifying exploitation of other people. Indeed, Saroyan, having now succeeded in winning Carol back, seems almost at once to have lost any genuine interest in an ongoing relationship.

The couple and their two children, along with the housekeeper-governess, lived together stormily in the house on Rodeo Drive for eight months, from March to October of 1951, at which time the marriage ended for the second and final time.

During this interval, Saroyan once again threw himself into a prodigious schedule of creative work—perhaps in itself a measure of his unease. He rented an office in Beverly Hills and simultaneously wrote three books: the first of his memoirs, *The Bicycle Rider in Beverly Hills* (1952); a stilted and deeply morose novel about a broken marriage entitled, with somewhat futile irony, *The Laughing Matter* (1953); and the quick, sometimes delightful, but overall rather glib fable, *Tracy's Tiger* (1951).

Saroyan's work was no longer selling as it once had; nor was it receiving the same kind of critical attention. Edmund Wilson had called a quotation from the last part of *The Adventures of Wesley Jackson* "surely some of the silliest nonsense ever published by a good writer,"[3] and from here on, although some of these later books were received more respectfully (Elizabeth Bowen praised *The Laughing Matter*), none was the occasion

Bill and Carol. New York. 1950.

Bill and Carol's second marriage. Los Angeles. 1951. From l. to r.: Ross and Armen Bagdasarian, Bill, Archbishop Calfayan, Carol, Araks and Manuel Tolegian.

of the critical or public excitement—whether an individual book was praised or not—that had been the hallmark of the early Saroyan.

HOWEVER, it was at this time that Saroyan had an unexpected windfall from the hit song "Come On-a My House" recorded by Rosemary Clooney, for which he shared cowriter credit with his cousin, Ross Bagdasarian, the son of Takoohi's sister, Verkine. In fact, the song had been all but entirely composed by Bagdasarian, Saroyan's junior by eleven years, when he was nineteen years old. Bill had only added a phrase or two later to the finished song. Indeed, at the beginning, Bill himself gave Ross complete credit for composing the song. Before Bill's second marriage to Carol, while the writer was staying in Los Angeles, he took Ross and Ross's wife, Armen, to a party at the Chaplins, and during the course of the evening Chaplin asked the young songwriter what he did. Ross replied that he and Bill had written a song together, and when Chaplin asked if he could hear it, Ross proceeded to sing "Come On-a My House" for him. Chaplin thought the song was wonderful, and Bill told him that it was entirely Ross's composition.

On the other hand, Saroyan did very little, if anything, to help his cousin break into the music business. He told Ross that it was a next-to-impossible undertaking and that it would be a waste of time for Saroyan to try to use his contacts to help him, which Ross had asked him to do. Ross had made a demonstration record of the song, and on his own he managed to get a copy of it to the singer Kay Armen, who then gave it to the arranger Mitch Miller—who, in turn, passed it along to Rosemary Clooney. She listened to Ross's version over and over again, and the recording of the song Clooney released duplicates the composer's phrasing word for word. This recording went on to make the charts even before Ross was aware that it had been cut.

At this point, Saroyan seems to have changed his mind, and he began to claim cowriting credit and royalties with his cousin for "Come On-a My House." There were even magazine and newspaper articles that referred to Saroyan as the song's sole composer. One evening, Chaplin reminded Bill of what he had said the night Ross had first sung the song for him. But Ross, for his part, genuinely wanted Bill to have cowriter credit for the song, as well as a full half of the royalties, in gratitude for the writer's encouragement in his early days. (Ross had appeared as the newsboy and later the pinball-machine addict in the original production of *The Time of Your Life*.) Significantly, however, Saroyan's name does not appear on any contract for the song.*

The Saroyans' second marriage ended one evening in a fight between Bill and Carol that escalated into violence—which, up to that time, Bill had avoided. On this particular evening, however, in a rage, he threw Carol down the stairs and then began to strangle her. Seven years old at the time, I can recall hearing a scream and running with my sister from the kitchen into the living room to find my father standing with his hands around my mother's throat. At the sight of Lucy and me, he dropped his hands. That same evening, Carol discharged the governess and, taking the children with her, moved out of the Rodeo Drive house. She borrowed several hundred dollars from her friend Martha (Stevenson) Goetz, and soon rented an apartment in Malibu.

A short time later, Bill had Carol served with a subpoena aimed at declaring her an unfit mother and taking the children away from her. Carol responded to this document by immediately phoning Bill and suggesting they meet to discuss the situation. At that meeting, Bill explained to Carol that if she wanted her freedom, giving up the children was the price she was going to have to pay. Rather buoyantly, he told her that unless she agreed to this, he would take legal action in which he would charge her with being insane and an atheist and declare that the woman she had hired as a governess for the children was a religious fanatic. As a consequence, she would then be asked to submit to an examination by a court-appointed psychiatrist.

Carol protested that Bill knew that none of his charges was true. Bill responded by saying that wasn't the point. The point was that the allegations would be made, and people would read them in the newspapers, and whether or not they were eventually proved false didn't matter, because all that people would remember would be what had been alleged against her. That was the way things worked, Bill told Carol with apparent

---

* Later in the fifties, Bagdasarian had another big hit with his own recording of his song "The Witchdoctor" and a more modest one with his instrumental, "Armen's Theme." Then, in the early sixties, the singer-composer, calling himself David Seville, had a success that turned into a multimedia phenomenon as the creator of the Singing Chipmunks.

delight in his own cunning. He repeated that if she wanted her freedom, the price would be letting him have custody of the children. It seems clear that, in this instance at least, Bill was less concerned with his children's welfare than with using them to inflict punishment on his wife.

Carol's next move is a clear indication that she was no longer willing to bow to Bill's tyranny. After she had made certain he actually intended to go through with his plan and she couldn't convince him to change his mind, she told Bill she was very sorry but, if this is what it came to, she would be forced to make a charge of her own. Otherwise, it seemed only too likely that the objectivity of a court-appointed psychiatrist might be swayed by the fact that Bill was a Pulitzer Prize-winning playwright.

She told Bill that if he filed false charges against her, she would be forced, in order to fight them from a credible position, to make a counter-charge and bring up his army history, specifically the fact that he had been confined for observation to a Section 8 ward. This stopped Bill dead in his tracks, and, though he was aghast at Carol for beating him at his own game, at the same time, perhaps a part of him grudgingly admired her fighting spirit. For if the writer was perfectly capable of the unsavory bullying he demonstrated here with Carol, he was also a man who doesn't seem to have been altogether sorry when someone called his bluff.

IN the couple's divorce settlement, against the advice of her lawyer, Jerry Geisler, Carol refused both alimony and community property. Bill was required only to send her $400 a month for child support. At the same time, largely from his "Come On-a My House" royalties, the writer put a down payment on a brand-new house in a development in Pacific Palisades, where Carol and Aram and Lucy were now to live. The house was bought in the two children's names, and the monthly mortgage payments of $175 were to come out of the child-support checks.

Simultaneously, Bill bought himself a small house on piers over the beach at Malibu. The Department of Internal Revenue was now hounding him for back taxes and, to avoid having a lien placed on the house, he bought it in his sister Cosette's name.

CAROL now found herself in the unfamiliar, and for her not very desirable, situation of being a young divorcée with two children, living in a neighborhood made up almost entirely of married couples and their families. Not inclined to aspire to a niche in the carpool or the PTA, she nevertheless managed to live for several years in this world before making another move. Aram and Lucy, in the meantime, were able to enjoy the benefits of the middle-class suburban neighborhood in which they found themselves.

During these years, Bill would periodically show up in the evenings about the time the kids were going to sleep, and he was sometimes able to coax his ex-wife into bed. A man had a need, he would explain, and Carol, rather desolately ensconced in a life she had never wanted, would on occasion accede to Bill's need.

I T was during this period that Carol began to write a novel about her early life with Rosheen and in foster homes; and at one point Bill lent her a typewriter. Then one afternoon when Bill was visiting, Aram came into the house from playing outside, and Carol asked him to wash his hands. For some reason, when Bill heard this, he told the boy, "Don't let her bother you, son." Having assumed almost the entire burden of responsibility for their children's day-to-day welfare, Carol became so enraged at Bill's undermining remark that she threw his typewriter at him.

"I don't want it," she yelled. "It only writes one thing, anyway."

"What's that?" Bill asked.

"'I love people . . . I love people . . . I love people . . .'" Carol chanted at him.

Bill would occasionally concede his own foibles with good humor, and this time he cracked up laughing.

I N the fall of 1955, *The Time of Your Life* was given a revival at City Center in Manhattan, and through Bill's influence, Carol was able to read for the part of Mary L, which she got. (In the same company, Gloria Vanderbilt played the role of Elsie Mandelspiegel.) During the rehearsals and for the run of the play, Cosette came to take care of Aram and Lucy at the house in the Palisades. In the meantime, Carol had also finished her novel, which was accepted for publication by Random House.

A S a result of these events, Carol eventually determined to move back to Manhattan with Aram and Lucy and try to make a new life for herself. At first, she and the two children lived in an apartment on Park Avenue,

OPPOSITE: *One of Saroyan's favorite photographs of Carol. Pacific Palisades. 1953.* (Photograph by Harold Halma.)

RIGHT: *Painting of Carol by Gloria Vanderbilt that Bill admired. 1956.*

BELOW: *Carol's photograph on the jacket of* The Secret in the Daisy. *New York. 1955.* (Photograph by Phyllis Cerf.)

which Rosheen, now separated from Charles Marcus, had taken. Then, after she and the children moved into an apartment of their own on East 93rd Street, Charles Marcus frequently gave Carol financial assistance. For with the move to New York, Bill became even more sporadic than he ordinarily was about sending monthly checks for child support, and Carol often had to depend on the generous credit extended to her by the neighborhood grocer to put food on the table.

Carol's novel, *The Secret in the Daisy* (1955), was well-received, and not long after its appearance she auditioned for and got a supporting role in the original Broadway production of George Axelrod's play, *Will Success Spoil Rock Hunter?* One of the leads in the hit play was performed by Walter Matthau, whom Carol would marry in 1959.

WHILE she and the children were still staying in Rosheen's apartment, Bill came to visit one evening. Carol was upset, for his sake, by a marked change in his appearance. For some reason, Bill had decided to have a nose-job and the results had been disastrous. Carol tried to play down her response to the surgery, for Bill himself was obviously aware it had been a fiasco. That evening, when the writer once again pressed Carol to go to bed with him, she agreed for what was to be the final time, largely because she sensed that if she refused he would think it was because of his appearance.

Bill eventually had a second surgery done, and the result this time was an improvement over the first operation. In addition, he now began to grow his mustache in a larger, walruslike style, which also helped offset the effects of the surgery.

11
NOT DYING

AFTER the failure of their second marriage and Carol's move with Aram and Lucy to Manhattan, Bill nursed a bitter grudge against his ex-wife. During the summer of 1957, when he took the two children to Europe, he regaled Aram with stories of what he regarded as Carol's duplicity, and returned the thirteen-year-old boy to his mother at the end of the summer after filling him with scorn for her—a scorn that Carol was now put to considerable pain to dispel.

THE following summer, Bill had the children fly to Los Angeles, where they lived in the Palisades house with a housekeeper Carol had employed in New York and on occasion with their Aunt Cosette. Bill stayed in his Malibu house but saw Aram and Lucy on a more or less daily basis.

Aram and Bill at a television studio. Los Angeles. 1953.

Aram and Bill at the World Series. New York. 1956.

Lucy and Aram. New York. 1956. (Photograph by Richard Avedon.)

Lucy Saroyan.

That July, Bill drove the children and Cosette up to San Francisco, where they stayed for several weeks in what had become, after Takoohi's death in 1950, Cosette's house. On the drive back, they visited Fresno, and, as they were driving around the vineyards near Malaga, Aram asked if they could stop to pick some grapes.

In a memoir published in 1962, entitled *Here Comes, There Goes, You Know Who*, Saroyan devotes most of a chapter called "The Time," one of the longest and possibly the most affecting in the book, to what now occurred.

After stopping the car, Bill ran into the vineyard and began to pick grapes. Then he noticed that Aram was just standing and looking. The fourteen-year-old boy said that he didn't think the grapes were ripe yet, and he didn't respond to Bill's promptings to pick some anyway. When Bill got into the car again, he was angry at Aram for asking him to stop but then refusing to join him in the vineyard to pick the grapes, even though he had done what Aram asked.

As he drove on, he bawled Aram out—and then Lucy, and even Cosette a little, too. Then, for an hour or more, nobody spoke. At this point, still baffled, Bill questioned Aram and learned that he was constipated and had a headache. Saroyan writes:

> I told him about myself when I had been his age. I had had nothing, but I had always been interested, fascinated even, by everything. On and on.
>
> I knew it at the time, I know it now, and I suppose he knew it, too: I was being angry at his mother.
>
> It was stupid, but I couldn't help it, that's all.[1]

They stopped for Cokes and the ride continued, while Bill helplessly continued to berate Aram, and sometimes Lucy, and occasionally Cosette again, too. The writer continues:

> At last the car began to climb the hills of Pacific Palisades, and soon we would be home.
>
> I was still going strong when suddenly my son said in a tone of voice that still hurts me, and has twice come to me in my sleep: "Papa, Papa, will you stop the car, please?"

I stopped the car, he leaped out, and in the very leap began to buckle and vomit, trying to hide behind a tree whose trunk was too narrow for hiding. The sound of his sickness sickened me. Once, twice, three times, four times, five times. Silence. His face was drained of color and covered with sweat.

Immediately after he had jumped out of the car my daughter jumped out, saying, "Aram, what's the matter? What's the matter, Aram?"

My sister said in Armenian, "You've made the poor boy sick. He isn't like you. He's like himself."[2]

The next day, however, Aram told Bill that it hadn't been his hollering that had made him sick, but other things. The writer concludes the episode:

I thanked him, but I didn't believe him, because I couldn't.

And my sister had been right in saying that he wasn't like me, only she'll never know how like him I was, but never vomited, because if I had, I might not be able to stop.

And I was sorry he wasn't like me, in that, because it is better not to get sick, it is better to find out how not to, it is better to insist on it, even, until it's almost impossible to get that sick, because getting sick doesn't get it, doesn't do it, at all.

But he hurt me, he hurt me deeper even than the failure and death of friends, and I loved him more than ever, and despised myself for never having been able to get sick that way, making him vomit for me forty years ago.[3]

There is a curious paradox here. In the penultimate paragraph, the writer declares the futility of allowing oneself to be sick. One even feels the swell of rhetoric as he proselytizes: "it is better not to get sick, it is better to find out how not to, it is better to insist on it, even, until it's almost impossible to get that sick . . ."[4] For better or worse, this is the prime lesson of the way Saroyan lived all his life: it is a rhetorical rallying cry on behalf of the psychological freeze discussed earlier. Yet immediately following this endorsement, Saroyan swiftly and accurately pinpoints one liability of holding to such a pattern. He clearly implies that a person who refuses to come to terms with his or her own history is, at least to some degree, condemned to perpetuate it—in Bill's case here, by making Aram sick. In fact, it is startling that the writer of the first paragraph, who unequivocally affirms such a life strategy, would immediately follow it with the self-excoriating "I . . . despised myself for never having been able to get sick that way, making him vomit for me forty years ago."[5]

But, in the end, perhaps the most telling comment is in the earlier paragraph where Saroyan tells us that he didn't vomit—"because if I had, I might not be able to stop."[6] Submitting to his own emotional condition meant for him, he makes clear here, the possibility of the permanent loss of self altogether.

Indeed, this is the central dilemma of the writer's whole life. Letting go—to himself or to others—seemingly threatened him with nothing short of personal extinction. That Saroyan would eventually grasp intellectually at least a part of the consequences of not letting himself explore his own emotional condition, makes it clear that, although he adhered to this pattern all his life, he did not do so out of anything so clear-cut as common obtusity. Indeed, the degree of self-awareness he demonstrates in the passages just quoted is reason enough for exercising caution when judging the writer's complex psychological pattern, rooted, as it seems to have been, in a wound he had received in the prerational depths of his three-year-old psyche.

IN his third and final phase as a writer, Saroyan produced a series of memoirs, turning from the autobiographical novel to clear-cut autobiography. These books, which include *Letters from 74 rue Taitbout* (1971), *Places Where I've Done Time* (1972), and *Chance Meetings* (1978), sold in the neighborhood of 10,000 copies each and were received with generally mixed reviews. Saroyan was now making his living primarily from his early writing, notably the paperback sales of *The Human Comedy* and *My Name Is Aram*, and royalties from performances of his most famous plays. But he continued to publish a book almost every year, switching publishers in this final phase with nearly every title. Although his American reputation and popularity had certainly slipped, he nevertheless continued to be dedicated to his craft—Michael J. Arlen tellingly characterized him in this period as an "artisan"[7]—and a number of these later memoirs contain excellent writing.

This autobiographical series began with *The Bicycle Rider in Beverly Hills*, written during his brief second marriage to Carol, but in spirit it might be said to have gotten genuinely underway with a book written eight years later, during the summer of 1959, which the writer spent with Aram and Lucy in Paris: a book he called *Not Dying*.

Not Dying is a curious work, not as effective as a number of Saroyan's later memoirs and troubled by a stylistic ambivalence: part interview, part autobiographical novel, part memoir. Yet, in its own way, it is a bold book, and one whose root concept, reflected in its title, serves as a kind of psychological bedrock for the later Saroyan, both as a man and an artist. In fact, the first chapter of this book is unique in exposing the levels of the writer's psychological reality.

Appropriately enough, it begins with the celebrated author being interviewed. This is the outward Saroyan, whose fame provides his primary social arena. The book opens:

> "And now, Mr. S.," the Interviewer said, "to what do you attribute your old age?"
> "Not dying. Is this interview for the *Paris Review*?"
> "No, this is for a paper in Dublin."
> "In that case, do I have your name right? Alakhalkhala?"
> "Why Alakhalkhala?"
> "A favorite name."[8]

Indeed, the fifty-year-old Saroyan scarcely cares to know who it is he is talking to—and the interview is soon reduced to an opportunity for displaying some of the writer's stylistic showmanship, which is wearing very thin now.

But then, unexpectedly, after scarcely half a page, the narrative takes a sudden jump. The interview is left off—there is a double space—and one encounters the writer at a deeper level than one can ever before remember encountering him:

> Six hours earlier, at eight in the morning, the night had begun to end in hot sunlight, with the birds of the trees just below the hotel window singing Jesus King Christ. And, singing, out of the bathroom came the slim body of the movie actress. (Well, didn't I first see her in the movies when I was twenty?) A week later at a play at the Gymnase a young girl in a fancy house was instructed by an old girl to flatter

her admirers by making a throaty noise, and the girl, misunderstanding a little, made the noise twice in a casual conversation, reminding him of the actress. Hell, he thought, it's an old trick, possibly out of the frozen North somewhere, a trick of the Eskimo girls, most likely.

Shall I write and ask her? Remember the throaty noises? What were they for? Togetherness? Being present? Not absent? Well, the night we met I had had five weeks of fighting off absence, which means becoming suddenly, unaccountably *out*, or nowhere.

In the stupid city of Cannes I nearly died in my sleep. My brother came there and smiled, as he'd smiled in the photograph taken (somewhere in California when he'd been six and I'd been three, his arm around my shoulder) by one of those traveling photographers of 1911, for which my mother, suddenly a widow, paid him a quarter. We had sat down on a broken sofa that had been moved out of the house and placed under a Chinaball tree in the weedy yard. It must have been in the town of Campbell, just outside of San Jose, where my father had just died. His dog, a white spitz with flashing eyes, stood directly in front of us, watching and waiting for any false move. Ready? And it was done. Forty-eight years ago. The Poet and his Brother. The Poet had his usual cold. His mouth was open because he couldn't draw air through his nostrils. His lips were dry, and there were two teeth marks in the middle of the lower lip. It was the Poet's eyes, though, that the traveling photographer had caught at the right moment. Wide open, fascinated, astonished, disbelieving.

Into the sleep of death and Europe my brother came, but why was he smiling that way? Hadn't I read in the *Scientific American* about a father in San Francisco who had suddenly stepped into a hotel room in New York to be with his son? They had said a few things to one another, and then the father had gone back to San Francisco, to his dead body there.

My brother said, "What have you done? Died?"

Me? What are you talking about?

But by then I was fighting for another chance.[9]

The vivid sensory detail of this writing, as well as its fluid shifts in time and space, motivated by the psychological continuity the writer is pursuing, may reflect the influence of the writers of the Beat Generation, especially Kerouac, who were at the time at the height of their vogue. Nonetheless, Saroyan, whom Kerouac himself credited as an early influence, moves into this stylistic territory with considerable mastery. If the rest of the book fails to live up to the promise of this first chapter, falling back on an episodic narrative involving Saroyan's summer with his children, this opening passage is of primary interest.

The writer has been fighting off death. At the same time, imperiled as he feels himself to be, he seems more susceptible than usual to the impressions of the physical world around him. Indeed, one would have to go back to the earliest stories, when Saroyan was a young writer so threatened by poverty that he scarcely knew whether he would survive as an artist at all, to find anything in his writing so vividly evocative as: "Six hours earlier, at eight in the morning, the night had begun to end in hot sunlight, with the birds of the trees just below the hotel window singing Jesus King Christ."[10]

Paradoxically, Saroyan is at the height of his powers as an artist at the very moment that he is presenting his sense of his own deepest vulnerability. As in his first story, "The Daring Young Man on the Flying Trapeze," there is a poetic quickening that occurs with the hovering imminence of literal extinction.

Next, a woman appears from the bathroom, like the birds below, singing—the woman, too, a part of the surrounding life in which the man feels himself to be threatened. Still, in the next moment, he expresses a certain suspicion with regard to her authenticity. Having identified her only as an actress, he goes on to question whether her "throaty noises" have been real or just a flattering performance on her part. He cannot quite trust the woman he is with—he isn't quite sure who she is.

Next, he tells of the specific circumstances of his recent skirmish with death: "In the stupid city of Cannes I nearly died in my sleep. My brother came there and smiled, as he'd smiled in the photograph taken . . ."[11]—and in another jump he moves back forty-eight years to the photograph taken immediately after his father's death, the event that was the primary death experience of Saroyan's life, when his own infant psyche had received its deepest trauma.

In his *General Introduction to Psychoanalysis*, Freud states: "An experience which we call traumatic is one which within a very short space of

Bill. Pacific Palisades. 1959. (Photograph by Aram Saroyan.)

Line drawing by William Saroyan.

time subjects the mind to such a very high increase of stimulation that assimilation or elaboration of it can no longer be effected by normal means, so that lasting disturbances must result in the distribution of the available energy of the mind."[12] As discussed in Chapter 1, there is some evidence that such an experience played a primary role in Saroyan's eventual decision to become a writer. At the same time, its consequences were to become increasingly apparent in his inability, as both a writer and a man, to sustain the give and take, light and dark, of a genuine relationship—and in his subsequent retreat into obsessive-compulsive habits, which may have acted as a "screen" for deeper anxieties.

The series of memoirs, in fact, might be considered one of the writer's final psychological mechanisms for dealing with his condition: one part of the complex of habits that was to dominate this final phase of his life. For over the years the writer had become, on a scale that suggests pathology, a collector.

SAROYAN did not so much furnish his houses and apartments as fill them with his collections: books, magazines, rocks, coins, and his own drawings and paintings (always signed and dated). He also kept old cigarette packages with one or two cigarettes left in them, hotel stationery, free pamphlets of every possible variety, matchbooks, and even used razor blade containers and old Vaseline jars. His houses were like encampments, makeshift arrangements of these objects. He seems to have found a healing comfort in their presence, and his various rooms could sometimes become almost impassable for the sheer mass of things he accumulated. But physical convenience and comfort were obviously not the writer's primary concerns; not, at any rate, when compared with what appears to have been the clearcut psychological need to have these things where he lived.

The writer's statement on the particular way he had determined to "outwit" death comes to mind: "it seemed to me that lasting things was the way to do it."[13] It is interesting to note that he doesn't say by *making* lasting things, that is, by specifically making works of writing that last. Rather, he makes a blanket statement that seemingly embraces anything at all that lasts. Here again is evidence of the materialism Saroyan displayed throughout his adult life and career. Perhaps the next question might be what the nature of this materialism is, that it could satisfy what appears to have been so deep a need in the writer.

To answer, one might first look at the problem he had in sustaining the deeper levels of relationship. For if his ego had failed to reach the fully functional level of development that would make sustained relationship possible, one result of this might be to severely limit Saroyan's sense of historical time: his sense, for instance, of the ongoing odyssey of his own and, by extension, of all human life.

Both as a man and a writer, Saroyan seems to have become almost a lifelong hostage to the legend of his own youth. The summer he wrote *Not Dying*, I came across a piece of paper on which he had written: "The only person I have ever really loved is Saroyan, and all that I really love now is the little of Saroyan still left in me." Again here is testimony, particularly poignant in this instance, that the writer could give greater weight to an abstraction—here, specifically, the literary persona of his youth—than to the actual moment-to-moment reality of his life. This being the case, it would be difficult for him to make the primary investment of time and energy necessary to develop and sustain a genuine human relationship. And hence he would more or less rule himself out of the fundamental process by which many read the deeper meaning of their lives.

But *things* would be less demanding. And, on a certain level, they might constitute an adequate substitute for a living relationship: they would in themselves comprise a kind of mute testimony to the passage of time in the writer's life. If for Saroyan there could be no marriage that would develop into the odyssey of discovery, both of the self and the other, that would then amount to one's deeper personal history, a collection of every issue of *Life* magazine, such as the one Saroyan kept during the years of his marriage, could provide a kind of alternative. It could exist as evidence for the passage of this actual time—and it would amount to *material* evidence. That is, it would have a physical weight and body to it that a relationship, strictly speaking, could not have. It would also be uniquely enduring. While a married couple's checkered history through good times and bad might disappear from the face of the earth leaving no visible trace, a sealed Mason jar with rocks in it would live on and on. It would be, perhaps, better than ordinary history—it would be a kind of immortality. Like Armenak's bundle of writings, it would remain.

Along with his own writings, published and unpublished, Saroyan's rocks and coins, his uniformly dated and signed drawings and paintings,

Saroyan's Paris apartment at 74 Rue Taitbout. (Dickran Kouymjian Photo Archive, Paris—Fresno.)

his hotel stationery, his pamphlets and his magazines, his cigarette packages and his old matchbooks are, in this sense, his history. They testify to his decision to live his life in enduring matter, as it were, rather than in the more demanding but perishable substance of living relationships.

Significantly, his memoirs after *Not Dying* make no attempt at sustained narrative—at chronological personal history—perhaps because, within the terms discussed here, Saroyan had none. Rather, the books are conceived as a series of episodes, no longer in any chronological sequence, in each of which the writer presents a story, an anecdote, a personality, or some combination thereof, that has remained in his memory. The books are like memory banks, each chapter representing a unique asset among the writer's holdings. In the end, the form itself is a kind of literary materialism: instead of a sealed Mason jar full of coins or a collection of old *Esquire* magazines, here is a more or less random selection of memories given permanent status as a published book.

12

THE WILLIAM SAROYAN FOUNDATION

IN the early sixties, Saroyan, now in his mid-fifties, bought a sixth-floor walk-up apartment at 74 rue Taitbout in the Opéra district in Paris. During the same period, he also purchased two new adjacent tract houses in a lower-middle-income development in his hometown, Fresno. Henceforth, Saroyan would divide his time between Paris and Fresno, for the most part spending spring and summer at his European pied-à-terre.

Both of these neighborhoods tended to isolate the writer. In Fresno, he was a famous, if rather eccentric, older man in a community of young families—and, as the neighborhood evolved, increasingly families of ethnic minorities. One of his houses was purchased specifically to provide storage space for his collections. The one next to it was for the writer himself. At a certain point, his neighbors, disturbed by the unkempt, weedy condition of his two front yards, complained to municipal authorities. Saroyan, who apparently preferred to cultivate outside his house the same kind of sanctuary for what people ordinarily discard as he cultivated inside, complied with his neighbors' wishes by hiring a gardener.

In Paris, where he alternately lived the final two decades of his life, Saroyan significantly made no effort at all to learn the French language. Perhaps as a result, it was in his rue Taitbout flat that he usually did most of his yearly published writing, although he seems to have written fairly constantly throughout his last years.

ABOUT the time he purchased these American and European dwellings, Saroyan first began to speak of a William Saroyan Foundation, or, alternately, of a William Saroyan Library. He seems to have been in search of a special building and property to serve as the final repository for all of his archives, artifacts, and other collections—a building he never, in fact, found. For a while, he also placed a small ad in literary periodicals for a qualified secretary to organize these materials. But he never hired anyone.

It may be surmised that the project of the Saroyan Foundation helped to focus the writer psychologically in his later years. His career had long ago leveled off so that, in spite of the fact that he published a new book almost yearly, many of those who had a more or less casual acquaintance with the writer's work were not sure whether he was still alive.

In the meantime, Saroyan's two children had grown up, and he did not have a close relationship with either of them. Indeed, his relationship with his children was much the same as it was with everyone else—in the deeper sense, distant. At one point, he discussed his plan for a Saroyan Foundation with Lucy, and made it clear to his daughter that he would not be leaving the substance of his estate to either her or Aram, but to his foundation. Lucy, in turn, gave her approval to his plan, if only to make it clear to her father that she didn't want to take anything from him.

Thus, in the final years of his life, Saroyan, who in his most famous play had had an old-world Arab repeatedly intone that there was "no foundation—all the way down the line," devoted himself to the idea of creating such a foundation—that is, a legal, tax-exempt, charitable foundation—that would bear his own name.

· · ·

H E chose to do this instead of allowing his estate to pass through the normal channels of mortal succession—specifically, instead of having it pass to his children. Saroyan's sense of his own integral place in a mortal chain of generations appears to have been very weak. Yet this wouldn't be inconsistent: for if the writer tended to identify more strongly with both the id (child) and the superego (in essence, the enduring wisdom of the race) than with the ego, his sense of the timeless and eternal would almost necessarily be more pronounced than his sense of the mortal and time-bound, essentially the province of the adult ego.

The foundation, then, was to provide for the care and maintenance not of Saroyan's children or grandchildren but of his *things*. He left his estate to his collections, rather than to his living heirs, apparently to avoid any sense of mortal impermanence. The terms of such a structure, which Saroyan created through his will, may also have reflected the writer's preference for inanimate things over living ones. Indeed, Saroyan lived at least the last two decades of his life mostly in the company of his collections; and his will, in turn, provides primarily for the care and maintenance of those collections. In fact, to avoid having his Paris apartment pass to his children—as it would have under French law—the writer took the deliberate measure of selling it to his foundation before his death.

In addition, there is a sense in which all the objects he provided for in his will are psychic artifacts that closely mirror—or more closely, in any case, than surviving heirs—his own psychological condition. If, in fact, Saroyan's developing psyche had been immobilized by his childhood trauma, a sealed Mason jar filled with rocks or coins might be construed as a symbolic representation of the "frozen assets" of the writer's deeper emotional life. If so, his obsessive concern with material things takes on a poignant personal significance: on a more or less unconscious level, he may have seen himself in them.

T H E fact that his literary archives would have most certainly fetched a handsome price from any one of many special collections libraries throughout the country, where they would have been catalogued and cared for by professionals and made available for scholars, critics, and biographers, does not seem to have deterred him from what appears to have been, under the circumstances, an unnecessary undertaking. It isn't certain, however, how much Saroyan knew of special collections libraries; nor is it altogether

*Saroyan at his will signing on October 21, 1980, in Fresno. His witnesses are
(standing, from left) Dr. Harold Haack, president of California State University at
Fresno; Dickran Kouymjian, coordinator of the Armenian Studies Program at
CSUF; Richard Harrington, Saroyan's lawyer at the time; (seated, from left) Leon
Peters, chairman of the Ad Hoc Steering Committee of the Armenian National
Museum; and Marvin Baxter, lawyer for the Armenian National Museum and
Cultural Center.* (Dickran Kouymjian Photo Archive, Paris—Fresno.)

implausible that he may even have entertained some private doubts that his work would be sought after by such libraries. Such doubts, of course, are patently absurd to anyone even slightly familiar with the special collections marketplace—which undoubtedly would have regarded the William Saroyan archive as a literary treasure. Nevertheless he began to make plans for the safekeeping of his collection at least fifteen years before his death.

The foundation was to maintain ownership of the papers and other collections, which were to be used for educational purposes. There was, however, a provision for parts of the collection to be lent to various interested institutions and libraries. All future royalties from the writer's work were to be used to maintain the writer's real estate properties and the following offices and officials of the foundation: an attorney, six foundation board members, and a literary executor (Kevin Starr, the writer and columnist for the *San Francisco Examiner*, was named to this position). If there was money left over after all of this had been taken care of, it was to go to provide scholarships in Saroyan's name for aspiring writers, with particular emphasis on young Armenian-American writers.

THERE can be little doubt that the William Saroyan Foundation was the writer's final bid for immortality. Surprisingly, however, it came not in the form of a culminating literary creation, but rather in the creation of a structure meant to "guarantee" by legal means that his name and his work would endure.

One can scarcely help being reminded by this of the title figure of Saroyan's early short story "Harry," the supersalesman who, even after his death, the writer tells us, was imagined to be "in heaven, or in hell, selling earthquake insurance . . ." It is almost as if the writer himself had, by the end of his life, come to resemble Harry, whom he hadn't quite made up his mind about at the beginning of his career. Indeed, the William Saroyan Foundation seems curiously like a lightheaded salesman's conception of immortality. In the end, it has about it the bullishly willful and at the same time rather sad air of someone trying to get God to sign on the dotted line.

13

LETTING GO

SAROYAN knew that he had cancer of the prostate at least two years before his death. During the spring of 1979, his old friend from the days of their Fresno boyhood together, "Yep" Frank Moradian, encouraged him to have the routine operation that would have effectively arrested this particular form of cancer. Moradian, president of the Penny Newman Grain Company of Fresno, even offered to have the operation arranged for in San Francisco, rather than in Fresno, if Bill wanted to avoid having his illness known in his hometown. But the writer protested that he had plans to attend a writer's conference in Eastern Europe and chose not to do anything about his condition. That same spring, scheduled to appear on the Johnny Carson Show, he didn't show up on the evening of the taping. He also failed to appear as the featured guest that summer at the Santa Barbara Writer's Conference. In both instances, Saroyan seems to have preferred to accept the invitations, knowing he might not feel up to making the appearances, rather than reveal his illness.

During the next two years, in which the writer changed the details of his will several times, the cancer made steady, and eventually irrevocable, progress. It spread from his prostate to his liver, and then went into his bones. By the morning of April 20, 1981, when the seventy-two-year-old Saroyan was found unconscious in his Fresno home by his cousin, Harry Bagdasarian, and subsequently was admitted to the Veterans Administration Hospital in Fresno, the cancer had apparently moved to his brain, inducing a coma. Unexpectedly, however, the writer regained consciousness overnight and didn't lose it again during the month remaining before his death.

T H E week before his admission to the hospital, his daughter, Lucy, whom he hadn't seen in seven years, drove up from Los Angeles to be with her father, after being informed of his illness by his Paris lawyer, Aram Kevorkian. Saroyan, however, who had mentioned to Kevorkian on April 11, 1981, the day he signed his final will, that if Lucy were in Fresno she could spend an hour or two a day with him, responded to his daughter's visit only by abusing her verbally, telling her to go after she had been inside his house a few minutes. He told her to tell Aram, too, not to come, not to write, and not to phone—that it would kill him if he did.

H A V I N G been given this information by my sister, I waited for two weeks before deciding that it was absolutely necessary for me to see my father before he died—whatever the consequences. In any case, by this time his doctor had informed me that my father himself now felt that the sooner he died the better, so that even if I did, in fact, hasten his death, it was apparently now a matter of indifference to him.

My seven-year-old daughter Cream and I drove down from Marin County to Fresno and spent approximately an hour and a half with my father in his hospital room on the afternoon of April 29. During this visit, we engaged in only a little conversation. There was a considerable amount of traffic through the room: a nurse was in and out repeatedly, and a doctor

Saroyan with his granddaughter, Cream. Bolinas, California. 1976. (Photograph by Aram Saroyan.)

Saroyan with his grandchildren. From l. to r.: Cream, Armenak, and Strawberry. Bolinas, California. 1977. (Photograph by Aram Saroyan.)

paid a visit—and my father spoke to them. Then, during the intervals in which the three of us were alone together, the room would once again grow quiet.

I sat down in a chair early on in the visit—parallel to my father propped up in his bed. My daughter eventually sat down as well, in a chair diagonally in front of his bed, so that, unlike me, she was easily in his range of vision.

I hadn't seen or communicated with my father for the past three and a half years. There was little for us to say to each other—we both knew there would be no way to straighten out our differences. I had come, essentially, simply to *see* him, to know firsthand that he was dying, and, if possible, to say goodbye to him.

Later in the visit, my daughter stood by his bedside and he held her hand—squeezing it gently, playing with her. The visit had quietly taken an unexpectedly warm turn. Then, after some time, his breathing indicated to me that he was asleep, and I got up from my chair and walked around to the far side of his bed, where Cream stood. There I saw that he had indeed fallen asleep, his face nestled between the side bars of his bed.

I suggested to Cream that she kiss her Grandpa goodbye, and she did, kissing the top of his head, on his hair, and at this point his eyes opened with a start. I now moved forward to kiss him goodbye. He looked up at me, then, as if bewildered by my coming forward, perhaps uncertain whether I meant to do him some harm. I had decided to kiss him on his forehead and as I bent forward to do this, I said, "Goodbye, Pop."

Suddenly, I felt my father's arm around my shoulder, and in the next instant, as he reached up, I found myself holding him in my arms. His body had been ravaged by cancer, and he was very light. The back of his neck, always firm and muscular, was now soft and relaxed.

"Thank you, Aram," he said, his voice deep with emotion.

"Thank *you*, Pop," I said, my own emotion suddenly swelling.

It was as if we were saying this both in the moment and, at the same time, for our whole lives.

Then he said, "It's the most beautiful time of my life . . . and death."

"For me too, Pop," I replied, now in tears.

As I held my father during those twenty seconds or so, I tried to communicate in my touch that I was strong and firm and at the same time gentle and easy. I had a vivid physical sensation that he was letting

William Saroyan. Fresno. March, 1981. (Photograph by Helen Minasian.)

go in my arms, melting and merging with me. Then, at the end, I laid him gently down on the bed and Cream and I walked out of his room.

As I was closing his door, now standing outside in the hospital corridor, I heard him exclaiming loudly to the empty room, "It's unbelievable! It's unbelievable!"

I had known my father during the second half of his life, the years of his decline, and until that moment in the hospital, I had never experienced a personal breakthrough of this emotional depth with him.

In considering how this moment came to pass, several things occur to me. First, he was once again, this time quite literally and irrevocably, in the grip of death: he knew absolutely that he was dying, and that quickening which occurred in him when he sensed his own mortality had now taken virtually final, full possession of him.

He had refused all the so-called "heroic measures"—the heavy medication with which cancer is customarily treated—and, aside from an occasional pain killer, was taking no medication at all. It was almost as if he were looking out of his eyes directly into the mystery of his whole life: the thing that had marked him almost from the outset, which was death itself. Indeed, I sensed that in those last days of his life, he was paradoxically engaged in the deepest unfolding of his own mortal experience. He knew he was going now, as his daring young man had known it, and he seemed to engage these final moments of his life with all the aspiring spirit and intelligence of the artist he had given every promise of being, without ever quite fulfilling that promise. During the visit with his doctor, he had said to him, in the slightly halting speech he had developed, striving to capture the thought itself, "I'm . . . letting go. Well, somebody said, maybe that's not the right thing to do. And I said—maybe it isn't. I don't know. I'm grappling with the mystery of . . . what . . . *is*."

It wasn't, after all, an easy thought. It wasn't his usual off-the-top brilliance, but a deeper questing after meaning that involved his whole being.

In the end, did he fling his arm around me and say thank you (those words he had always so resisted) at least partly because, as a dying man, he knew he wouldn't have to take responsibility for the emotional opening between us, and would never need to commit himself to the harder work of sustaining it? Perhaps so.

For me, of course, it scarcely matters why or how it happened. In the end, I am left gratefully amazed that, at long last and entirely unexpectedly, it happened at all.

WHEN he died two and a half weeks later, the Associated Press released his "last words," which, in fact, he had phoned into their Fresno office the week before he fell unconscious and was admitted to the hospital. The words, which quickly went around the world on the wire services, were: "Everybody has got to die, but I have always believed an exception would be made in my case. Now what?"

The irrepressible old song-and-dance man, even at death's door. The charm of a last joke. Yet he may only have believed so strongly in his own immortality because his access to the deeper realms of mortal experience had been frozen as a consequence of his childhood trauma.

If this was so, when he regained consciousness in his hospital room, it was as if those long-frozen corridors of his deeper emotional life had gone into a final thaw. And when I came to see him, for the first time he *let* me see him down past all our previous thresholds; and the emotion his generous parting gesture brought out of me joined his own emotion and traveled back and forth through us both.

As I closed his door, standing in the hospital corridor, and heard him shouting "It's unbelievable! It's unbelievable,!" it was as if he had just attained some unforeseen emotional vista, one that challenged all the assumptions he had held up to that very moment. In the end, it was a different kind of immortality, after all, that we had suddenly come upon that afternoon: the paradoxically mortal kind called love.

AFTER his death on the morning of May 18, 1981, William Saroyan's body was released to the Fresno chapter of the Neptune Society, who carried out the stipulation of his will that he be immediately cremated with no funeral services. The will further directed that his ashes be delivered to the trustees of the William Saroyan Foundation, and that, if possible, one half of those ashes subsequently be delivered by the trustees to an appropriate location in Armenia.

BIBLIOGRAPHY
PLAYS
NOTES
INDEX

BIBLIOGRAPHY

.   .   .

The Daring Young Man on the Flying Trapeze and Other Stories. New York: Random House, 1934.

Inhale and Exhale. New York: Random House, 1936.

Three Times Three. Los Angeles: The Conference Press, 1936.

Little Children. New York: Harcourt, Brace, 1937.

Love, Here Is My Hat and Other Short Romances. New York: Modern Age Books, 1938.

The Trouble with Tigers. New York: Harcourt, Brace, 1938.

Peace, It's Wonderful. New York: Starling Press, 1939.

My Name Is Aram. New York: Harcourt Brace, 1940.

Three Plays (My Heart's in the Highlands, The Time of Your Life, Love's Old Sweet Song). New York: Harcourt, Brace, 1940.

Three Plays (The Beautiful People, Sweeney in the Trees, Across the Board on Tomorrow Morning). New York: Harcourt, Brace, 1941.

Saroyan's Fables. New York: Harcourt, Brace, 1941.

Razzle-Dazzle. New York: Harcourt, Brace, 1942.

The Human Comedy. New York: Harcourt, Brace, 1943.

Get Away Old Man. New York: Harcourt, Brace, 1944.

Dear Baby. New York: Harcourt, Brace, 1944.

The Adventures of Wesley Jackson. New York: Harcourt, Brace, 1946.

Jim Dandy: Fat Man in a Famine. New York: Harcourt, Brace, 1947.

The Saroyan Special. New York: Harcourt, Brace, 1948.

Don't Go Away Mad and Other Plays. New York: Harcourt, Brace, 1949.

The Twin Adventures. New York: Harcourt, Brace, 1950.

The Assyrian and Other Stories. New York: Harcourt, Brace, 1950.

Rock Wagram. New York: Doubleday, 1951.

Tracy's Tiger. New York: Doubleday, 1951.

The Bicycle Rider in Beverly Hills. New York: Scribner's, 1952.

The Laughing Matter. New York: Doubleday, 1953.

The Whole Voyald and Other Stories. Boston: Little, Brown, 1956.

Mama I Love You. Boston: Little, Brown, 1956.

Papa You're Crazy. Boston: Little, Brown, 1957.

The Cave Dwellers. New York: Putnam, 1958.

William Saroyan Reader. New York: Braziller, 1958.

Here Comes, There Goes, You Know Who. New York: Simon and Schuster, 1961.

Boys and Girls Together. New York: Harcourt, Brace and World, 1963.

Not Dying. New York: Harcourt, Brace and World, 1963.

One Day in the Afternoon of the World. New York: Harcourt, Brace and World, 1964.

After Thirty Years: The Daring Young Man on the Flying Trapeze. New York: Harcourt, Brace and World, 1964.

Short Drive, Sweet Chariot. New York: Phaedra, 1966.

I Used To Believe I Had Forever, Now I'm Not So Sure. New York: Cowles, 1968.

The Dogs, or the Paris Comedy, and Two Other Plays. New York: Phaedra, 1969.

Letters from 74 rue Taitbout. New York: New American Library, 1971.

Places Where I've Done Time. New York: Praeger, 1972.

Days of Life and Death and Escape to the Moon. New York: Dial, 1973.

Sons Come & Go, Mothers Hang in Forever. New York: McGraw-Hill, 1976.

Chance Meetings. New York: Norton, 1978.

Obituaries. Berkeley: Creative Arts, 1979.

PLAYS

. . .

My Heart's in the Highlands (April 1939)
The Time of Your Life (October 1939)
A Theme in the Life of the Great American Goof, a ballet play (1940)
Love's Old Sweet Song (April 1940)
The Beautiful People (April 1941)
Across the Board on Tomorrow Morning and *Talking to You* (August 1942)
Hello Out There (September 1942)
Get Away Old Man (November 1943)
The *Cave Dwellers* (October 1957)

Dates given are for the first New York productions.

NOTES

· · ·

PREFACE

1. *New York Times*, May 19, 1981.
2. *Manchester Guardian*, May 19, 1981.
3. *Los Angeles Times*, May 22, 1981.
4. *New York Times*, May 19, 1981.

CHAPTER ONE

1. William Saroyan, "The Daring Young Man on the Flying Trapeze," in *The Daring Young Man on the Flying Trapeze and Other Stories* (New York: Random House, 1934). Reprinted by The Modern Library (New York: 1941), p. 25.

CHAPTER TWO

1. "The Daring Young Man on the Flying Trapeze," p. 19.
2. Ibid., p. 17.
3. Ibid., p. 20.
4. Ibid., p. 23.
5. Ibid.
6. Ibid., pp. 24–25.
7. Ibid., p. 18.
8. William Saroyan, "Seventy Thousand Assyrians," in *The Daring Young Man on the Flying Trapeze and Other Stories* (New York: The Modern Library, 1941), p. 179.
9. William Saroyan, "Harry," in *The Daring Young Man on the Flying Trapeze and Other Stories* (New York: The Modern Library, 1941), p. 179.
10. Ibid., p. 181.
11. Ibid., p. 180.
12. Ibid.
13. Ibid., p. 184.
14. Ibid., p. 188.
15. Ibid., pp. 188–189.

CHAPTER THREE

1. William Saroyan, *Sons Come & Go, Mothers Hang in Forever* (New York: McGraw-Hill, 1976), pp. 22–23.
2. William Saroyan, *One Day in the Afternoon of the World* (New York: Harcourt, Brace and World, 1964), p. 72.
3. William Saroyan, *The Trouble with Tigers* (New York: Harcourt, Brace, 1938).
4. William Saroyan, *Love, Here Is My Hat* (New York: Modern Age Books, 1938).
5. William Saroyan, *My Name Is Aram* (New York: Harcourt, Brace, 1940), p. 3.
6. James Agee, *Agee on Film*, Volume 1 (New York: McDowell, Oblensky, 1958–60), pp. 387–388.

CHAPTER FOUR

1. William Saroyan, *Boys and Girls Together* (New York: Harcourt, Brace and World, 1963), pp. 33–34.
2. Ibid.
3. Ibid.

CHAPTER SIX

1. Edmund Wilson, "William Saroyan and His Darling Old Providence," in *Classics and Commercials: A Literary Chronicle of the Forties* (New York: Farrar, Straus, 1950), p. 328.
2. Ibid.
3. Ibid., pp. 328–329.
4. Irwin Shaw, *New York Times Book Review*, June 2, 1946, p. 1.
5. *New York Times*, May 19, 1981.

CHAPTER SEVEN

1. William Saroyan, *The Time of Your Life*, in *Sixteen Famous American Plays* (New York: The Modern Library, 1941), p. 918.
2. Wilson, "William Saroyan and His Darling Old Providence," pp. 327–328.

CHAPTER NINE

1. William Saroyan, *Rock Wagram* (New York: Doubleday, 1951), pp. 1–2.
2. William Saroyan, *Papa You're Crazy* (Boston: Atlantic-Little Brown, 1957), p. 151.

CHAPTER TEN

1. Maya Pines, "New Focus on Narcissism Offers Analysts Insight into Grandiosity and Emptiness," *New York Times* (March 16, 1982), C1.
2. William S. Appleton, M.D., *Fathers & Daughters* (New York: Doubleday, 1981).
3. Wilson, "William Saroyan and His Darling Old Providence," p. 330.

CHAPTER ELEVEN

1. William Saroyan, *Here Comes, There Goes, You Know Who* (New York: Simon and Schuster, 1961), p. 255.
2. Ibid., pp. 256–257.
3. Ibid., pp. 257–258.
4. Ibid., p. 257.
5. Ibid., p. 258.
6. Ibid., p. 257.
7. Michael J. Arlen, interview with Robert Cromie on "Book Beat," National Educational Television, 1975.

8. William Saroyan, *Not Dying* (New York: Harcourt, Brace and World, 1963), p. 3.
9. Ibid., pp. 3–5.
10. Ibid.
11. Ibid.
12. Sigmund Freud, *A General Introduction to Psychoanalysis* (New York: Washington Square Press, 1960), p. 286.
13. William Saroyan, "Growing Up In Fresno," recorded interview, California State University at Fresno, February 1976.

INDEX

ABOUT THE AUTHOR

*Aram Saroyan was born in New York
and now lives in Bolinas, California,
with his wife and their three children.
He has written several volumes of poetry and
is both an essayist and the author of
an autobiographical novel,* The Street.
His most recent book, Last Rites, *also deals
with his father, William Saroyan.*

DATE D